To Act, To Do, To Perform

THEATER: Theory/Text/Performance

Enoch Brater, Series Editor
University of Michigan

To Act, To Do, To Perform

Drama and the Phenomenology of Action

ALICE RAYNER

Ann Arbor

THE UNIVERSITY OF MICHIGAN PRESS

1997   1996   1995   4   3   2

A CIP catalogue record for this book is available from the British Library.

Library of Congress Cataloging-in-Publication Data

Rayner, Alice.
    To act, to do, to perform : drama and the phenomenology of action
/ Alice Rayner.
       p.   cm. — (Theater—theory/text/performance)
    Includes bibliographical references (p. 157–61) and index.
    ISBN 0-472-10537-X (alk. paper)
    1. Drama. 2. Act (Philosophy) in literature.   I. Title.
II. Series.
PN1647.R39   1994
792'.01—dc20   94-3828
                                                                    CIP

Contents

Acknowledgments

There are many people who will see the effects of their help in this book, and I cannot hope to give them sufficient thanks. Each one deserves a story apart. It was Robert Cohen's production of *Hamlet* at the University of California, Irvine and the student who played the gravedigger that set me to thinking about a single line from the play and its implications for the whole. John Gronbeck-Tedesco gave me great encouragement by publishing the essay "Grammatic Action and the Art of Tautology" in *Journal of Dramatic Theory and Criticism,* an essay that has expanded into two chapters here.

Responses from students at various stages have led me continually to rethink and rework, and I am most grateful to Miranda Joseph and Lance Miller for their insightful comments on early chapters; Miranda was good enough to see the political implications in the abstract theory. Jarrett Walker read an especially unwieldy draft and asked the pertinent questions that helped to shape the whole. I am very lucky to have worked on related dissertations with Zander Brietzke and David Saltz, whose work was so pertinent to my own. Brietzke's "Nothing Is but What Is Not: Chekhovian Drama and the Crisis of Representation" has thoroughly explored the artifice of Chekhov's realism, an issue that I only touch upon in my chapter on Chekhov. Saltz's "The Reality of the Theatre Event: Logical Foundations of Dramatic Performance" rigorously examines the use of a game model of action and places it in the context of aesthetics, with a similar aim of breaking down false dichotomies in the concepts of action on the stage. David also gave the manuscript a careful proofreading in a tight time schedule. I am most grateful to them both and know they will see the fruits of our exchanges here.

To Charles R. Lyons I owe special thanks for seeing my work through a long process. He read this manuscript at various stages and gave me the benefit of his tact and insight. His knack for seeing what it needed without intruding upon the development of my own ideas has been a great gift.

The influence of Bert O. States will be clear to anyone who knows his work, but he cannot be blamed for either the influence or the shortcomings of the book. As a teacher, he gave me the happy sense of discovering ideas independently when in fact they had been there long before, and I can't think of a better way to learn what phenomenology might be. As a reader, he has encouraged me to keep my theoretical excursions in perspective, the text in view, and the voice my own. He has been an extraordinary mentor.

For pulling the manuscript out of virtual reality after hard-disk crash, I owe thanks to Ron Davies in the Stanford Department of Drama. His computer expertise is impressive, but his extraordinary good will and apparently tireless care for making the manuscript presentable are incalculable. LeAnn Fields, Executive Editor at the University of Michigan Press, has given me support and encouragement for this project and I am extremely grateful for her sustained efforts in seeing it through.

Finally, it is friends and relations who have given me the support to complete this project. My sisters Jeanne and Betsy have encouraged me throughout the long process. To Bill and Sue Rayner, Mike, Kristen, and Kelly, I owe thanks for summer refuge at Lake Tahoe and long discussions on the specific mysteries of procrastination and the uncanniness of change. Jonathan Berkeley has helped me keep various distortions in perspective. Tom Caldarola has given friendly readings and long-term support in the bleaker moments. Lastly, my son, Eric Quandt, has been my model for the solution to the theoretical problems I outline here. He continues to show me grace in action.

Introduction

This book investigates the phenomenon of action. It began when I tried to understand a line in *Hamlet* in which the clown identifies three branches of an act: to act, to do, and to perform. Initially, the line seemed to be a useful way of talking about the problem that Hamlet was having all along: how to move from an idea of an act into action and how to account for the change. At the same time, it was a nice joke. The apparent analysis of an act into its parts was turned into a useless tautology by the clown's logic. The combination of analytic categories and tautology, however, gradually appeared as a contradiction that became basic to my understanding of action itself. For if the terms *act, do,* and *perform* are truly self-defining, why have different words? What do those differences identify if those words are virtually interchangeable? In discussing one term, the others almost necessarily come into play so that even while trying to draw conceptual differences and to anatomize action into constituent parts, I found it difficult to sustain their differences except in the most theoretical way. Practical action, in other words, is conceptually divisible but in pragmatic terms would appear to be one thing that, precisely because it is practical, marks the difference between mental and material fields. The contradiction between the analytic division and the self-defining terms suggested to me that within action there may indeed be both a system of differences that keeps it open to redescription and a tautological element that makes action a unitary, self-representational system. It is a combination that finds its way into the theater.

In pursuing the line from *Hamlet*, I realized, furthermore, that I was taking this understanding from the action I saw taking place in grammar and began to consider how grammar might be a place where the problems of action were lurking. Since the project itself came from a play obsessed by the problem of action, I wondered whether that grammatical field had any relation to the dramatic one and decided to use the grammatic as an entry to the dramatic. As I saw the simultaneous openness and closure of action as the combination of discursive, material, and performative dimensions, I considered how the representation of the problem in *Hamlet* (and the other plays where the difficulties are represented) might be used to identify the dismantling of action in a performative present, when a representation or discursive structure approaches the purely performative or tautological dimension. That is, could the problems that certain dramatic characters have in relation to action illuminate action's appearance over and against its own absence and demonstrate its dissolution in the very moment of performance? How does the representation of such a problem in a character like Hamlet intersect with or identify the apparent contradictions in the relation of text to performance, or drama to theater?

The first task was to identify the problem. What eventually became clear is that one problem is the word itself. The term *action* may apply on the one hand to virtually anything that moves and on the other hand to a conceptual frame that expressly limits what counts as action. A full sense of action, then, would need to take the variations in usage into account. In its limited sense the idea of action is predicated on the volition of an intending subject, distinguishing an act from mere motion or from accidental, involuntary, or nonhuman events. This narrow definition, common to law and philosophy but identified similarly from Aristotle to Lacan as a structure of intention,[1] has a number of consequences, one of which is to make an act a construction of language in which an act is identical to the articulation or name: hence it is a self-representation, conditioned by the position and ideology of a speaker of the word. Action is a language problem. When, for example, one responds to the question "What are you doing?" the answer "I'm taking out the garbage" identifies the act but does not include either all the particularities and contexts involved or all the other possible designations of the act, such as "I'm cleaning up your mess." On the other hand, more general sense of action can refer to anything that moves, like the action of a motor or a watch, suggesting a purely physical dimension. In some contexts, the word *action* distinguishes the sense of actuality from mere ideas, separating the sense of "really" doing something from just thinking about it. Here, action is a motion problem. It operates like a differential between the mental and the physical. But thinking and speaking can be actions. The problems become even more complex as the idea of action implicates questions of volition, the position of a subject in action, the intersection of speaking and doing.

Reductive methods relating to philosophy and law have had consequences in the history of dramatic literature and criticism, where it is customary to see a radical separation between text and performance, between the conceptual and the actual, and between the relatively permanent written artifact and the transient theatrical enactment. These divisions have interests in common with the methods of philosophy and law. They similarly limit the definition and conceptual framework for regarding action in order to categorize and judge. Analytic philosophy in particular seeks to determine the minimal number of elements that comprise a basic action, in order to identify its essential characteristics and structure. The law of the court as well as the culture needs a similar reduction of action to its intentional features because legal and social consequences depend upon identifying the voluntary, motivational intent of an agent, as distinct from circumstances beyond the control of the agent. The separation between thinking and doing, and analogously between mind and body or text and performance, persists.

In this book I want to expand rather than reduce the concept of action and to indicate what Gilbert Ryle might call its "thickness." But that thick description will be in the form of a scheme taken from the gravedigger's speech. This will necessarily include discussion of the elements of intention, as well as the act of framing an act, but in addition to intention as a distinguishing feature, I want to propose a way of conceptualizing action that includes those features occurring in *practice*, which modify the idea that an agent or subject exists prior to or behind its action. The project involves a reversal of the conventional Aristotelian idea that drama is the medium of action. Instead, I want to consider action itself as a medium with its own conflicting tendencies and to examine those conflicts and contradictions. Action, in other words, is the field that lends its discursive, material, and social characteristics to the context of theater. The discussion will not, therefore, describe performances in particular, theatrical practices, or actual events as they occur on the stage but will include an idea of performance as one dimension of action itself.

Initially this means outlining how the distinctiveness of action does involve attributing intentions to agents, but I hope to indicate how that attribution is deeply embedded in a linguistic construction that has grammatical form, implying further that notions of action give evidence for ideologies of responsibility. To name the act, say, *suicide*, or *revenge*, is one way to assign blame or innocence, to give identity to an agent and to assess an ethical situation. The substantive noun that identifies the act and abstracts it into a name is nonetheless embedded in material practices. Action is a field in which the substantive object and the transitory process intersect, interact, and provide correctives to each other. These are issues I will examine in chapters 1 and 2, "Gravedigger as Theorist" and "To Act: 'Did That Never Happen to You?'" While there is no perfect conformity between the linguistic, the conceptual, the practical, and the social, no dimension can exclude the other. The disconformities in concert with the identifications give an act both openness and closure.

The interplay of these dimensions comprises the phenomenal complexity of action. In other terms, action can be understood as an intersection between abstract points of the *name* of the act, its actuality, and its social context. The challenge is to find the language that can describe such interplay when language itself is the source of the abstraction. I want to break down the notion that action is an object to be theorized and applied to specific practices, and to map a territory of the grounds for understanding action in action. Each chapter stands to some degree on its own, but together, I hope, they encircle questions of how action produces subjects in process and how process is the condition that reveals the temporal dimensions of subjects in action. Such process is, on the one hand, held in suspense by the fixations on the abstract idea or name of the act, and, on the other, independent of the fixations of the subject's consciousness. The question of action, then, centers around the placement of consciousness and attention toward time itself and asks for the dissolution of fixed ideas of act and subject. Emile Benveniste points out,

> An opposition between "process" and "object" cannot have a universal validity, a fixed criterion, or even a clear meaning in linguistics. The reason for this is that notions like process or object do not reproduce objective characteristics of reality but result from an expression of reality which is itself linguistic, and this expression can only have a limited validity.[2]

Linguistically, there are words that resolve the opposition, in the sense that they can function as both nouns and verbs. When such a word functions in one position as an object, it nevertheless carries in the background the force of the other, as process. *Play* is such a word. In both function and designation, moreover, play indicates a solution for the restless interaction between the parts of action itself.

The literature on play, like that on action, is vast. From Huizinga to Derrida the concept of play obviously has widely diverse uses: from the basis of all cultural institutions for Huizinga to the endlessness of the signifying process for Derrida. But among the common elements in its usage is the sense that it is both a structure and an instance, a reiteration of rules and a self-representation, both closed by a regulated system and open to accident and improvisation. It sustains the sense of motion and moment.[3] Wolfgang Iser has indicated that "asking what, exactly, play is, tends to make it disappear, since such questions only try to make play represent something other than itself."[4] And as Hans-Georg Gadamer has suggested, the distinction between reality and the aesthetic does not hold in the field of play. He argues that play, or the aesthetic, is not a modification of reality but an instance of it, just as Benveniste indicates that the distinction between object and process is primarily a linguistic one. So with action: the construction of an act gives it form and structure in such a way that it can be repeated: the construct confers identity. Such identity, however, is only conceptual because it is apart from enactment. But an act without a name is no act. Put another way, structure becomes actual in material and temporal moments, but a pure present cannot be grasped. Play is a word that incorporates both dimensions. If the play of action is the medium for drama and theater (not *of* them) then performance need not be understood either as an embodiment *of* a text or a freedom from textuality or structure. The genitive case there has too long been taken in its derivative sense.[5] The same genitive case has a unifying aspect, such that the performed action is not a derivation or duplication but something made in and by action, something that is both praxis and poiesis, something relentlessly visible and conceptual.

That there are difficulties in the relationship between object and process, text and performance, structure and play, however, becomes especially apparent when an agent or subject appears to have trouble negotiating between the name of the act and the practice.

This trouble is especially visible in *Hamlet,* which is one reason that play will dominate this book. For one persistent issue in the phenomenon of action is where and how a subject/agent is positioned in it. Is the subject a cause or starting point? Is it a product or object? How do motive and motion relate? How does the intending agent conform to the name of the act? How does the interiority of intention inhibit the performance of an act?

Each chapter will examine a possible position for an agent or subject in relation to acts, as that position is revealed by a grammatical structure. While this will involve some play analysis, I am making no pretense of analyzing the plays or even the action of plays and their development completely; nor am I trying to outline a theory for all dramatic and theatrical practices or literature. The range of plays I discuss is distinctly narrow, in part because the discussion is dense rather than wide-ranging and in part because these plays in particular seem to me to represent the issues of action while they enact them. On the other hand, no chapter is meant simply to demonstrate a theory. Together, rather, they comprise a scheme or anatomy of action. The first chapter outlines categories for a conceptual framework. Each of the following three highlights the distinctiveness of one of the categories, while the fifth suggests their synthesis, in which the interplay of elements gives an act its reality. If the result is inconclusive, that is because it seems to me that any conclusion about the truth of any given action is itself an exercise of power, conditioned by ideology, over the radical indeterminacy of time. While determinations of the truth or meaning of an action are inevitable, if not necessary, and while they become embedded in history and culture as part of the symbolic nature of action, which is part of what constitutes it, I am interested in keeping its radical indeterminacy in the forefront.

By using dramatic texts, I want to indicate something of the multiple nature of action: at once a signified object, a process of signifying, a material and temporal present, and a playing. Each of these further involves a subject, or *actant,* and an implied observer. To claim that these dimensions are simultaneous in drama is to say that there is little real distinction between the action represented and the action *of* representation. The use of these texts in particular allows me to "thicken" the relation between representation and "real" action. Thus, I am using drama as an instance of *virtual* action, to show how and where *real* action is recognized, shaped, and interpreted.

Drama in performance employs each of the three areas mentioned above: it is textual, material, and public. As Bruce Wilshire has put it, "theatre as phenomenology is a fictive variation of human relationships and of human acts *in act*. Theatre should not be regarded as contemplation set over against action and creation, but as contemplation through action and creation."[6] Understandings and experiences about the nature of an act, that is, exhibit both epistemological and ethical constructions of human behavior.

Drama and theater, however, are not necessarily identical. While drama may be said to shape action and theater to make it visible, action itself is the medial realm composed of both shape and visibility. Dramatic texts serve to reinforce the dimension of action as representation where *theater* and *performance* offer the dimensions of its visibility and actuality.

The first chapter, "Gravedigger as Theorist," takes a line from *Hamlet* to set out a conceptual map for the territories of action that are named there as "act, do and perform," which indicate differentials within the field. This chapter outlines a range that sees action in its dimensions as a noun, a verb, and an adverb, analogous to its conceptual, temporal, and qualitative features. The conceptual is substantive, making the act appear as a thing that seems to abide through time; the temporal, as I describe it, is both physical and of the present, where it has no duration; and the qualitative is a relational dimension, in which the act is in play within a complex system of cultural pleasure and libidinal exchange that can be called, in brief, *style*. The focus on style as the perceptible phenomenon serves to displace the subject-centered structure of the act, turning the agent from its position as simply a volitional subject, whose intentions are the sole determinants of deeds, into something closer to a manifestation of qualities. With this perspective, the act and agent are not set out as substantive things with attributed qualities, because qualities themselves constitute the phenomenon. As the most general discussion, this chapter could serve as much for a conclusion as for an introduction.

I discuss the grammar of the act, as conceptual, retrospective, narrative, and repeatable in the second chapter, where I assert the active-passive structure of an act in a discussion of Estragon and his boot in *Waiting for Godot*. In this aspect, the act is a noun or the *name* of itself. The chapter is an investigation of how notions of intentional

action are themselves already representations of an act and how they
are therefore already available for repetition and duplication in the
form of narrative and identity. Specifically, I propose that the linguistic
model of a volitional act invites re-representation because it is
already a construction in which a volitional subject is turned into a
passive object from whence it derives identity. The collapse of active
and passive voices in dramatic representation puts the subject between
assertion and passion, suffering the effects of its acts in a
tautology. The chapter explores how a subject becomes textual and
tragic. It takes Kenneth Burke's notion of the tragic dialectic of active/
passive but suggests how that dialectic goes beyond an Aristotelian
notion of tragedy toward a phenomenal description of action itself.

In the third chapter I discuss how the extremity of doing, which
is the irreducible present and material manifestation of action, involves
a disintegration of the conceptual dimension; how the name
dissolves in time and the subject cannot be identified as an object.
The example for such dissolution is Macbeth, whose reach is toward
an apocalyptic presence. This is the aspect of the verb that combines
a sense of motion with a sense of actuality and a present in which
past and future combine as a totality. At an extreme, apart from the
repeatable name of the act and the social determinants of quality, the
materiality and pure presence of doing function demonically, as they
do in *Macbeth*. The chapter on *Macbeth* explores the way that the
present makes itself known as pure visibility, resisting negotiations
with both past and future, but attempting to become all one, all at
once.

In the fourth chapter I use some characters in Chekhov to illustrate
the differences between subject-agents inhibited by the demands
implied by the concept of an act and those who are more
clearly performers, able to play the moment without defined identity,
intention, or purpose. This chapter on *The Three Sisters* looks at how
inaction is the result of a construction of a subject-agent as an extreme
interiority. The psychological interiority of the sisters can be understood
as one consequence of the assumption that a subject is fully
constituted prior to its acts. The private, psychological subjects who
cannot move contrast with other Chekhovian characters who demonstrate
the exterior, public, and social aspects of performance. Both
pragmatists and players in Chekhov present a stark contrast to those

who are *only* volitional or desiring and whose desire makes it impossible for them to work or get to Moscow.

The final chapter returns to *Hamlet* to suggest how the performative, play, and replay of action functions to dissolve the substantive-attributive concept of the act by replacing the name of the act with style or quality. The opposition between object and process becomes a cooperative opposition. The structure makes what Gadamer calls a "meaningful whole," but the structure itself is made actual only in terms of the qualities manifested by enactment. *Hamlet* exhibits the way that these dimensions—act, do, and perform—function recursively, each modifying and informing the others. The text is revived by *doing* it, but doing it also creates a past and a textuality and an identity in retrospect. The doing of the text is itself an act that is both retrospective and prospective, looking both toward the finished object and the open possibility for as yet undiscovered interpretations in the public domain. In *Hamlet* it is possible, furthermore, to see how such recursive action involves the negation of the *name* of a subject. That is, while a negative seems to be a purely linguistic phenomenon, a subject too can be manifest as a negative both in a refusal or resistance to action and in a displacement of volition.[7]

Rather than a volitional structure, action is shown as an interplay of qualities. Those qualities, adverbial in nature, are not attributes of the act, but the act itself, in its performative, erotic dimension. Quality or style is not an attribute, at least once the notion of a substantive act—an act as a thing—is subordinated to the actuality of appearances. Instead of looking at an act as a thing, one can look at the qualities of appearances as the site of action. In the dissolution of the belief in an act as an object, quality becomes the performative exhibition of action in progress, manifesting as play and interplay among rules, subjects, actors, and audiences.

One of the underlying questions that I address by indirection until the last chapter is exactly *how* it is possible to move into action, given its several parts: Hamlet's problem. The means or manner for action—its style—arises on the site of the combination of parts, between them, at their intersection and interaction, with the participation of an agent in circumstances beyond its making, in the act of making an unseen structure visible in a public arena.

I recognize that in many ways the scheme implies more than it explicates and incurs the dangers of a phenomenological approach that only "uncovers the obvious." It is perhaps shockingly ahistorical for the consideration of a phenomenon that is always and emphatically in history and subject to the texture and variation of cultural climates. Obviously *Hamlet*, *Waiting for Godot*, and *The Three Sisters* emerge from radically different sets of cultural values, languages, and performative moments. But one of the functions of the anatomy as opposed to historical description is to indicate the categories or areas that any specific historical analysis would need to take into account. The problem of action, moreover, is a repetitious one; new in each instance, it is the same but not identical to other instances. The point is to identify the problem that is being repeated and to relocate the site where we look for it. I hope to imply by the methodology of the book that theory need not be something directly applied to aesthetic works like a poultice but is something that emerges from such works, which are already ways of seeing. The questions that emerge from the art of action, moreover, point to the limiting factors in both art and action as they engage a sense of the real. The joke of the gravedigger, finally, must remain intact: parodying analytic method itself and turning it into a comic performance of a logical proof with mutually defining terms. For taking the implications further and finding the uses of schematic fiction, I rely on the reader to extend this performance and remember that the conceptual framework is based on the words of a gravedigging clown.

Chapter 1

Gravedigger as Theorist

It must be [*se offendendo*]; it cannot be else. For here lies the point: if I drown myself wittingly, it argues an act, and an act hath three branches—it is to act, to do, and to perform; [argal], she drowned herself wittingly. (*Hamlet* 5.1.8–11)[1]

Although they are already in the process of burying her, the clowning gravediggers, laboring like critics, are concerned to account for Ophelia's death. Did Ophelia commit suicide? The answer has consequences. A suicide cannot be buried in consecrated ground. Shall we offer praise or blame? What happened? How do we judge the act?

The answer requires a careful and discerning legal mind. The coroner, according to the gravedigger, has made such a decision about Ophelia: he has "sate on her and finds it a Christian burial." "How can that be, unless she drowned herself in her own defense?" asks clown one. The other replies: "Why, 'tis found so." The judgment on Ophelia, like the one on Hamlet and on *Hamlet* that will follow, is passed only when there is a corpse, after the action has become a thing of memory. " 'But is this law?' 'Ay marry, is't—crowner's quest law' " (5.1.19–20). Ophelia's action is held up to the standards of the law, indicating how the meaning of an act has it sources and its consequences in social and juridical systems, interpretive codes and contexts. There can be as many disagreements about that meaning as there are articles on *Hamlet*, but in each case, the corpse will be buried by the gravediggers.

The clown's view of Ophelia's death, however, is a useful outline for multiple perspectives on an act. Unlike the coroner, he is neutral. His only job is to dig the grave. To him, it does not matter whether Ophelia drowned wittingly or unwittingly, whether she went to the water or the water came to her. A corpse is a corpse. As a theorist he articulates the structure of action divorced from a living context, suitable largely for a grave, not unlike the task of analytic philosophy.[2] As a dramatic character, however, he places the analysis in the context of a dramatic action. I hope to illustrate how the clown is a theorist of action who recognizes the analytic divisions or parts of an act and a phenomenologist who participates in the tautological self-identity of an act. If the clown were a real philosopher, one might have to take his analysis as final or complete, but by the fact that he is already a fictional figure, he contextualizes his analytic act in the act of digging a grave, an act that is virtual on the page, actual on stage.[3]

The three branches, he says, are: to act, to do, and to perform. The line is also a joke. If one were concerned that all the spoofing of academic pretentiousness in *Hamlet* had been murdered with Polonius, the clown brings back the verbal ghost of the old counselor reminding us of a certain emptiness and impotence in logical forms.[4] The line resounds with pretensions of Aristotelian analysis, in which the parts are mutually defining terms. Using the formalities of logical proof, the clown proves by tautological definition that an act is an act is an act and at the same time proves himself a rustic who does not know how to make a logical form *get* somewhere. The proof is essentially meaningless because it is tautological, yet as Harry Levin points out, it "rings the changes on a momentous word."[5] Those mutually defining terms are nonetheless distinct, and an examination of their difference provides not only an analysis of an act but a description of three distinct *perspectives* on the act. For the three branches are also three views, three means of conceptualizing the positions of intentionality, materiality, and performativity. A complete sense of an act, that is, needs to account for the position of the agent, for the material facts of a deed, for the discursive or rhetorical formulations that implicate an audience or world in the act itself and that give it qualities. It would need to account for praxis and kinesis as well as the rhetorical and formal constructs by which they are perceived. And it would further need to put these parts into something like a recursive system in which each informed and qualified the other. What follows is a series of propositions about how these three branches might be distinctive.

To Act

Intention, from Aristotle onward, is an "animating" principle, distinguishing act from event, praxis from kinesis. If Ophelia intended to
kill herself, then her act is suicide; if she happened to drown when
all she intended was to sing her song while floating downstream,
then she did not commit suicide. If she is in no condition to intend
anything, she is likewise innocent. In the latter case, the law will
render compassionate judgment upon her act and allow her Christian
burial. If she intended to drown, she is an agent at the origin of the
act—the cause—and she will be buried beyond the Christian pale.
Intention differentiates voluntary from involuntary action and from
mere motion. That distinction has specific social uses by assigning
responsibility to an agent in the context of social, legal, and codified
standards.

The notion of intention does more than describe some inherent
principle that sets objects in motion.[6] It is, first, the ground upon
which social institutions and cultural epistemes determine what Fou-
cault named as the discipline and punishment, the sanction and ta-
boo, as well as the sympathy or abhorrence that follows upon any
individual act. In this framework, the act is an ethical event, and a
specifically social one. It cannot, as a result, be exempt from the
rhetorical strategies by which intention is attributed and meaning
conferred; it cannot escape the perspective of the onlookers. Sec-
ondly, in the traditional view, intention is related to form, a form
that in Aristotle's terms has a beginning, middle, and end, is whole
and complete, and thus is defined by its retrospective view and its
repeatability. In this, it is aligned with narrative.

The idea of the voluntary links the practical, juridical field of
action and the fictional field. That linkage accounts for the common
correlation between drama and the law, in which human acts are
tested or put on trial to judge the relation between agents, deeds, and
social norms. The recognition of mitigating circumstances, of conditions beyond the control of an agent, allows that the deed alone is
not sufficient to condemn but must be considered in context. That
context, in Western tradition at least, is answered both by the "what,
why, who, how, with whom or against whom."[7] What counts for
adultery in Peoria may not be what counts in Elsinore; and what

counts as burial in Forest Lawn may not be what counts on stage. In consideration of that context, the trial examines not only the motive of the agent but also the naming of the act. As Aristotle put it,

> Now it often happens that a man will admit an act, but will not admit the prosecutor's label for the act nor the facts which that label implies. He will admit he took a thing but not that he stole it. (1374a1)

This is an argument Falstaff might well approve when he asserts that running away from Gadshill was not an act of cowardice but an act of recognition of the True Prince. The meaning of the act, in other words, is an assertion. Above all, that assertion assigns a name. It claims that the name of the act derives from motive, from thought processes or states of mind, from circumstances within the control of the agent. The name, however, pretending to transparency, conceals the fact that it *is* an assignment. It appears as a natural rather than a social state and hides the power dynamics that sustain the social authority for naming, cloaking the position and power of whoever speaks the name. It is this dimension of action that has been subject to the major criticisms of poststructuralist, psychoanalytic, and feminist theory. The struggle for the authority to name is at the heart of most political, moral, and social crises. For the moment, however, I simply want to identify the dimension of action that continues to take intentions into account without yet exploring how the critiques usefully question the very foundations for the constructions of identity of an act and a subject. Those foundations lie in the historical sedimentations and ideologies of responsibility. The critiques of power, that is, cannot wholly escape what Paul Ricoeur calls the "conceptual network" that distinguishes action from physical motion.[8]

    This network—who, what, when, where, and why—applies equally to law and fiction. It furthermore correlates fictional descriptions of circumstances to a pre-figured concept of agents and deeds, and that correlation, to Ricoeur, is mimetic. Some of the less radical critiques of the subject and the act, one might say, fill in the areas of this network with new names but keep the structure. The idea of voluntary action at some level is at the root of an evaluation of acts, even when those acts are shown in the context of involuntary conditions. Notions of both fictional character and real-world identity derive in part from assumptions about the freedom to choose, from assumptions about what constitutes motive and cause, from ideas of responsibility or victimization.

It is of course impossible to say, in the context of *Hamlet*, that Ophelia chose to die: there is evidence that she is not in a condition to choose and, most certainly, she is constrained to some extent by a script. But this is in part how her character is delineated. Even in allowing that her act is not voluntary, the perception of the act is already installed in a volitional context, regardless of its fictional status, and therefore in an ethical one. Mimesis, in this view, is an ethical accounting, not simply a reflection or imitation. The mimetic is not something inherent in the act therefore, nor is it simply a mirror of some absent or other reality; it is instead the place at which the perception of acts adheres to prior assumptions about the relation of agents and acts and the proportions between voluntary and involuntary. Ophelia, as a textual construct, is of course no more than a hypothesis, but she, like other characters, carries along other facets of what Bert States has called "mimetic interests," which "require that there be something verisimilar ('like us') about the motivational basis of character action and speech."[9] It is not necessary to reach a final judgment, because Ophelia is in a play, not a courtroom. The freedom of the fiction allows the complexity of her situation to rest as a complexity: it engages the ambiguities of the circumstances, so that her death can be seen as neither voluntary nor involuntary, but rather as fitting to the circumstances.

There are traces of such ethical interests even in explicitly nonmimetic forms. When Heiner Müller deconstructs Ophelia in *Hamletmachine*, he refocuses that mimetic interest onto the context of the history of textuality and representation. But the image of an Ophelia bound in a wheelchair, ranting, maintains a sense of Ophelia as an involuntary agent in the history of representation, tied to forms of representation, still not free to act as an independent, autonomous "person." Müller thus continues to some extent to demonstrate the ethical site at which the possibility for the autonomy of personhood, where agents *could* attach voluntarily with their acts, is in conflict with restricted conditions, which in that case are textual, historical, and cultural productions of *Hamlet*. The effectiveness of the image of Ophelia, in other words, still relies on a set of attitudes and values concerning voluntary and involuntary, freedom and constraint. However much *Hamletmachine* unravels the conventional perceptions of the relation of agents and acts and of character, it still relies on the persistence and cultural history of ethical relations. For even if it is impossible to imagine the motives of Müller's Ophelia or to attribute any psychological underpinnings to the behavior of the figure on stage, as for a conventional character, we nonetheless can neither be affected by her image nor find it intelligible without some sense that it is horrific to be bound and deprived of voluntary motion.

The notion of intention also conditions certain formal properties in the perception of action. If one imagines that Ophelia is the origin and cause of her own death, she determines a cohesion between beginning and end. Her act is teleological and describes the linear trajectory between intentions and goals.[10] The temporal relation between intentions and goals has pervaded the persistent commonsense notion of action in the Western tradition. Motive is a *beginning*, and thought is a strategy. Both are presumed to be prior to activity or motion. Aristotelian tradition disallows an infinite regress of causality by relating a desire to a beginning point and an end, as though desire or intent were a wholly voluntary, rational *thing* at the origin of action. This model in fact constructs a sense of linear time, or time as a series of points on a line: action begins where thought leaves off.[11] Like the name, linear narrative form pretends to transparency, obscuring its own framing devices and offering a view of a supposedly natural act.

The connection here with the Aristotelian notion of plot is obvious. Aristotle locates causality at the site of intentions that are the motivational and ethical source for strategies of thought aimed at a goal. Plot can be an imitation of action in this view because it purportedly shares the same temporal structure: action itself is already, inherently plotted into beginning, middle, and end, and the consonance between beginning and end of the plot is *already* analogous to the teleological structure of desire. That structure is the basis for Peter Brooks's description of plot in *Reading for the Plot*. He says there "that narrative has something to do with time-boundedness, and that plot is the internal logic of the discourse of mortality."[12] This would locate a theory of action within a theory of narrative in which all action is similarly directed toward death, or with endings as analogues to death. It suggests that the telling itself is primarily the pleasurable delay of the inevitable end. And to the extent that action involves humans or representations of humans, the premise is perhaps irrefutable, for all action does eventually end in death and occurs with death in sight.

The alignment of action and narrative then assumes that an act is predicated on the paradigm of the individual life span. As theorists from Benjamin to Kermode, Todorov, and Brooks have pointed out, the prospect of death and ending already shapes a retrospective view on actions. The relation of acts to ending and completion is what makes narrative and repetition possible. To act is therefore also the Oedipal dimension of an action in the sense that the Oedipus narrative is the paradigm of intentional action that shapes meaning and identity as a formal arrangement of time.

Every moment in Sophocles' play is a development of Oedipus's stated intent to find the murderer of Laius. With every step forward toward the discovery there is a symmetrical step backward toward the discovery of who he was and always had been. The Oedipal plot completes the inquiry with a recognition of the simultaneity of past and present. Oedipus's action is mimetic not because it refers to an absent, true act but because it appears to coalesce with a set of possibilities from the temporal field analogous to an individual's span between birth and death. Such death directedness in the narrative form that Brooks discusses, in which death is the sanction of meaning, is the object of many of the criticisms of narrative form. Teresa de Lauretis, for example, asks specifically what kinds of things that form excludes and answers that the voice of the woman, the Sphinx, is left on the margins.[13] The Oedipal narrative of Sophocles' play has nothing left over or on the margins. It makes the life of Oedipus a total form that describes the shape of self-awareness and self-knowledge, unifying past and present through the unfolding investigation. Time and identity are constituted by the form. Narrative in effect is not a reflection but a creation of how they are known; but as de Lauretis and others have pointed out, it also excludes alternative constructions and suppresses other voices.

To a great extent an act is perceptible because of a set of interests that determine which behaviors are significantly attached to a whole. That delimiting notion of *an* act, in short, already depends upon a notion of plotting, of choosing coherence and meanings, of assigning ownership, responsibility or causality to events, however much the ownership may be in dispute. Even to conceive of an act therefore implies a consciousness that sees not the myriad and possibly extraneous motions and behaviors common to rocks and other bodies in motion, but the thematic intentionality that appears to *cause* motion. The perception of *an* act is therefore also a learned perception.

The distinction between motion and action, however, has important consequences and helps to identify this branch of action as a specifically social and political phenomenon. For George Herbert Mead, the social context is definitive of both the act and the self, which arises out of what he calls the "conversation of social gestures."[14] Unlike the Aristotelian idea that the self is fully constituted prior to acts, Mead insists that selves "are constituted by or in terms of the social process."[15] The social context of action in part provides the resistance that the individual organism encounters; that external resistance is gradually internalized as a developing self anticipates such resistance and learns to resist on its own. In *A Grammar of Motives*, Kenneth Burke, interpreting Mead, points out that

> a social relation is established between the individual and external things or other people, since the individual learns to anticipate their attitudes toward him. He thus, to a degree, becomes aware of *himself* in terms of *them* (or generally, in terms of the "other").[16]

"Self-criticism," says Mead, "is essentially social criticism, and behavior controlled by self-criticism is essentially behavior controlled socially.... Hence social control ... [is] actually constitutive of and inextricably associated with that individuality."[17] Social interests, that is, become the terms by which the individual becomes conscious of a self. An action, in this view, is evidence of the position of the individual relative to the symbolic codes of the culture: self-aware either through conformity or resistance to those codes. The self is thus as contextual as its acts.

Beyond the competence of a preunderstanding of a relation between acts and agent, Ricoeur recognizes the mediation of the "symbolic resources" in the field of practical action. In brief, taking a cue from the anthropology of Clifford Geertz, Ricoeur notes the relative valuation of actions in the signs, rules, and norms assigned by symbolic, cultural values.[18] Fiction or narrative, in other words, is not free of a real world. The scene, to use Kenneth Burke's word, is not just an inert receptacle for goings on but symbolic negotiation between the representations of action and the cultural values in which it occurs. The scene in the broadest sense is the site of reception, not just the representation of a situation. Culture is the terrain that determines both what it is possible for a given agent in a given epoch to do, and the judgments, values, and meanings that occur in relation to other agents in other times. The differences in scenes are the poles of any given hermeneutic circle. This dimension is what Reiner Schürmann calls "the practical a priori."

> In any given age, everyone has a preliminary knowledge of what it is economically possible to do. . . . Such knowledge comes to us primarily from our hands, for example, from the tools epochally at our disposal. No one in the Stone Age dreams of a stainless steel axe nor, conversely, of a wooden plough in the age of mechanized agriculture. No one in the Greek polis imagines organized lobbying of a federal legislature, nor is direct deliberation feasible in a mass democracy. The implicit understanding of an economy springs from what we make and do.[19]

This practical a priori extends to the symbolic a priori, between the real and the fictional. That certain kinds of acts have meaning is already evidence of symbolic manipulation. How the relation of agents and acts is formed is thus a kind of technology for making ethical evaluations. At issue is how we understand and project context and scene not as part of agents' intents and desires but as part of the "circumstances they did not make."[20] For both fictional and historical characters, those circumstances include the historical moment of reception. Thus, Oedipus's act, like Pericles', will necessarily mean something different to fifth-century Athens and twentieth-century United States.

Phenomenology has obviously played a major role among the critiques of a naturalized sense of action. In a discussion with Hans-Georg Gadamer, for example, Ricoeur aligned a theory of action with

a theory of narrative and insisted that action is largely understood
not as a pure instance of an intending agent but as a text or narrative
that necessarily includes the position of an onlooker.

> The intersection between the theory of texts and the theory of
> action becomes more obvious when the point of view of the
> onlooker is added to that of the agent, because the onlooker will
> not only consider action in terms of its motive, but also in terms
> of its consequences, perhaps of its unintended consequences. . . .
> Detached from its agent, a course of action acquires an autonomy
> similar to the semantic autonomy of a text. It leaves its mark on
> the course of events and eventually it becomes sedimented into
> social institutions. Human action has become archive and docu-
> ment.[21]

The teleological form of intentional action positions the judge or
namer of the act outside the act. Indeed, to some extent it presumes
the presence of a judging consciousness that, like the coroner of
Hamlet, will make a finding on the case, for that judgment is the
self-defining purpose of delineating an act in the first place. What
such a position and such a form exclude, obviously, is the relativity
principle that is brought back into action by theatrical enactment. It
conceals the fact that the observer is inevitably not only *in medias res*
but also in the middle of its meaning as well: philosophers, like audiences, cannot escape the effects of their presence with the object. The
theater audience, furthermore, manifests an instance of the fact that
human action, no matter how private, always occurs in a social and
historical context. The audience is not in that context, it is part of the
context and therefore partially constitutes the structure of the act.

The act in Ricoeur's terms is a sedimentation whose living fluid-
ity is congealed because it is narrative and therefore repeatable. In
this dimension, it is a corpse that is revivified in the act of retelling
or reenacting. That reenactment is a part of the performance dimension that I will discuss further on. At this point, it is simply enough
to reiterate the way in which the conceptualization of an act, through
which it is known and understood, first requires its death. Ophelia's
act is thus archival, inert evidence of what was once a living context.
The coroners of cultural institutions render judgments upon it, rein-

forcing their own power and authority, but they cannot revive her. The coroners themselves, as in the history of criticism, indicate the status of law and convention for any given moment in history more than the truth of her death.

To Do

What is it, exactly, that Ophelia did? She had been onstage, showing signs of insightful madness, but there is only Gertrude's report of her death. Gertrude says that Ophelia wove flower garlands, tried to hang them on pendant boughs, fell into the weeping brook, and was carried away, singing hymns. From this it would certainly seem that she did not "seek her own salvation." What she did could be described with more objectivity than Gertrude provides, however, cutting through the poetry to facts. Such objectivity could assume a wide range of specificity. What comprises objective facts is certainly open to debate, but had a camera been pointed at Ophelia, it is doubtful that we would be directed to think about the "pendant boughs" or "weedy trophies" or a "weeping brook": we would simply see them. As Seymour Chatman defined the difference, the camera "names" while the verbal "asserts."[22]

The difficulty in describing an event objectively illustrates how hard it is to see facts apart from their verbal evaluation. But we take it for granted that Ophelia went through certain motions and died. Is it possible to separate Gertrude's valuation of Ophelia's act from its fact? Probably not. But there are alternative systems for the valuation.

One indicator for the distinction between acting and doing might be found in Wittgenstein's question, "What is left over if I subtract the fact that my arm goes up from the fact that I raise my arm?" [23] If to act is the dimension of action that links acts and intents, then to do might be said to sever intentions and regard only the material or gestural conditions. The relation between the two is not unlike that between language and the body. The body is not free of inscription, but neither is it identical to inscription. In psychoanalytic vocabulary following Lacan, the body is an object that is other than the speaking subject. The "I" who speaks is not coextensive with its materiality or the "me." The subject is not identical to a self or person. For the present purposes, the difference between them, the subtraction, concerns both the visibility of the body as an object and the temporality of its actions and is a difference between praxis and kinesis.

Things happen, in other words, but not always are they caused by a person; not always can we assign responsibility, and not always can we understand them in terms of the human psychology of intent, wish, belief. This category of materiality considers among other things the distinctiveness of motion and objects. Motion is a capacity common to animate as well as inanimate objects. Like kinetic energy, it relates to the physics of energy, force, and change through space and time: it is common to humans, rocks, stars, planets, trees, the Humboldt current, hedgehogs, arms, legs, arrows, bourgeois capitalism, needles on the Richter scale, keyboards, bullets, hares and tortoises, light switches, trains, wheels, dancers, the Dow Jones average: in short, to things.

In that sense, the matter of the body can be associated with fatality. This is first because the body is born and will die. Second, it is because the living body is in a constant present or here and now that is inescapable until death. But it is also because the body is "other" to language and speech. It remains implicated in speech and inscription but is resolutely not identical to them. The body is object to the speaking subject and has a separate set of capacities and constraints, like a mechanism that contradicts spoken or conscious intents. The body has a mind of its own and speaks its own kind of language, like the Lacanian unconscious. But it speaks of the actual in distinction to the ideal, of the present, not of the past or future.

From the perspective of doing, the body is an object in motion. It requires a perception of its thingliness. To see the distinctiveness of doing would be to perceive the motion of the body in isolation from a person, as when one no longer observes someone walking but sees a walk. To see doing is to perceive nothing but thingliness and see a street full of walks rather than people and their dogs. This disassociation between thing and sign is the perception that created Sartre's *Nausea*. It also comprises the basic usefulness of Victor Shklovsky's idea of defamiliarization or of Brecht's idea of *Verfremdungseffekt*, which takes things out of their familiar context in order to see them as things or, equally, to see the system in which they appear as natural. The understanding of motion, for example, is predicated on the isolation of movement from any intentions and a prior network of institutional, social values. Though it is most easily comprehended in terms of material world, motion is also conceivable within abstract systems such as capitalist economy or a cultural apparatus. In fact motion is perhaps best understood in terms of systematic change insofar as it is necessary to factor out what is sometimes loosely called the human element, which is another name for intentions, desires, or context. Motion belongs to the thingly or impersonal realm when we study it but is the most specifically physical when we "do" it. It can thus be well described by graphs and formulas, objectively, as manifest behavior.

The verb *do* furthermore emphasizes not the context or content of an action but the sense of its actuality. It is a remarkably empty verb: it can be filled with any number of specific qualities and references to specific actions, but its force is to cite the sense of material reality and presence in distinction to the hypothetical, rhetorical, or possible. Its temporality contradicts and confounds the repeatability that the tellable dimension of the act allows, for *to do*, with its emphasis on the actual, is unrepeatable. The quality of actuality derives from that one-time-only aspect, the here and now. *To do* functions as if there were only a present and as if it were only consciousness that complicated matters by an awareness of past and future. It is thus a radically nonmimetic act, more characteristic of avant-garde performance art, say, than of literary form.

Doing does not have the kind of linear temporality of Aristotelian action because it is not shaped by the extension between intentions and ends, with a delay in the middle. For both performer and audience the temporality is the same. In doing there is no dilatory space or delay. At most, the intention and the gesture are simultaneous and therefore shapeless. Doing is emphatically in the present and has no duration through time. Though it may take time, it does not make time, insofar as it has no residue. It thus requires no pre-, con-, or re-figuring of time: doing is the figuring itself. What Ophelia does, supposedly, is lie down in the river: death and judgment merely follow upon the deed. Doing can thus be aligned with epic time rather than tragic, for it concerns events more than intentional actions, and epic is the form for relating deeds. The annal is perhaps the closest historical record of doing in the way that it exhibits a peculiar kind of emptiness in pure facticity, as though there were no context for facts. As Hayden White describes the annal:

It possesses none of the attributes that we normally think of as
a story: no central subject, no well-marked beginning, middle,
and end, no peripeteia, and no identifiable narrative voice . . .
there is no suggestion of any necessary connection between one
event and another. . . . Social events are apparently as incomprehensible as natural events. They seem to have the same order of
importance or unimportance. They seem merely to have *occurred*,
and their importance seems to be indistinguishable from the fact
that they were recorded. . . . And recorded *by whom*, we have no
idea; nor any idea of *when* they were recorded.[24]

The historical record of doing thus has an emptiness similar to
raw data. Perhaps an athlete is the clearest example of what I mean.
Statistics are particularly useful in describing what an athlete does.
We might suppose that any baseball player intends to hit a home run
on demand, and most are capable of it at some time or other. But the
statistics show up elements that have little to do with the players'
conscious intentions. Statistics indicate norms of behavior that say
Eric Quandt, for example, does not hit low and inside pitches; that
he "likes" high and outside at a count of three balls and one strike;
facts that he himself may not know until the statistics say so, and
that he may even want to deny. Statistics tell not what players think
they intend but what their bodies intend, which is what they *do*.
Statistics are unforgiving in their description of the actual deeds. The
consciousness involved in doing, in distinction to intention, has a
direct kinship with the athlete, who must suspend conscious thought
and let bodily skills take over, allowing for the possibility that the
body has a mind of its own.
    Doing in the sense of motion is at once more fundamental and
more abstract than action, which involves rhetoric and ethics, deliberation and delay and specific qualities. We say, for example, that
babies and animals can perceive motion but do not necessarily know
what it is that is moving; yet once the baby or the dog learns by
experience that one particular motion ends up meaning *food*, it is
more difficult to perceive the motion or sound in itself without the
association with its meaning. Indeed, it takes extra concentration to
eliminate associational meanings from motion, sound, and sight and
to perceive sensations in themselves: motion and its qualities need
to be subtracted from its learned, contextual meanings. Motion is

thus a rather advanced concept: a phenomenon that is at once obvious and concealed by conceptual habits. It requires an unlearning
and a re-viewing. It requires a divorce between intentions, desires,
and symbolic codes and a reconfiguration according to other systems.
Put another way, if *to act* were identical to *to do*, there might never
be any failure of either intention or motion.

Like nature, motion is always there in some sense, but it is necessary to learn that such and such a perception is motion in the same
way Monsieur Jourdain learned he had been speaking prose all
along. We may think that all along we have seen people walking, but
really we have always also been seeing walks. Acting teachers, likewise, know how difficult it is for students to unlearn their concepts
and to concentrate solely on motions, and any number of exercises
focus on suspending consciousness or putting consciousness into the
physical. The student trained in naturalism asks why this character
walks. At one level that is an appropriate question; at another, the
teacher or director says, don't ask, just *do* it, because discoveries
about emotion, attitude, even reasons often occur as a *result* of doing,
not before doing. In the dimension of doing, it is possible to learn
about the deed, to describe it in a scientific sort of way, to make an
act into an object.

When doing occurs in isolation from soul, ethics, and rhetoric,
we are in the realm of the pure force common to beasts, machines,
or automatons who appear to operate without autonomous will. This,
at least, is the Cartesian distinction between human action and that
of animals and machines. The machine or automaton, for Descartes,
could never be human since, like an animal, it had no interiority, no
will or soul, though one could confuse the two if judged by exterior
motion alone. "We base our judgment solely on the resemblance
between some exterior actions of animals and our own; but this is
not at all a sufficient basis to prove that there is any resemblance
between the corresponding interior actions."[25] But this is exactly the
point: exteriority is the site of visible motion where doing is seen.

The physical and material dimension of action can, on occasion,
be divorced from the rhetorical, moral, or affective conditions. Such
separation was the goal of Dada experiments in the early twentieth
century or of John Cage's games with chance later on. The early
operas of Robert Wilson are in some sense pure doings that are ar-
ranged on principles more formal than ethical. Human bodies are

almost wholly figural images in his work. That is: the difference between acting and doing can be aesthetically manipulated to the extent that the intentional and affective elements may disappear entirely. Kleist, in his essay on the puppet theater, notes a greater capacity for grace in the puppet than the human, for the puppet is not affected. "For affectation appears, as you know, when the soul is found at any point other than the movement's center of gravity. . . . Of course . . . the spirit cannot err where there is none."[26] The affective behavior of the human, with its "disorders of consciousness," inhibits and distorts the physical behavior of the body-as-machine, where the puppet is free of such disorders and is subject only to laws of physics. Similarly, if human intention aims at control of chance in the realm of ethical acts, John Cage conversely tried to make those chance operations apparent, as pure event.

Doing, even in its recorded form, whether annals or images, resists the intelligibility of the act. It does not create a narrative form for knowledge, judgment, and comprehensibility because it occurs in a kind of temporal collapse as raw data. It is both purer and less comprehensible in terms of narration. It is the record that "the arm goes up" with the subtraction of "I raise my arm." The knowledge that is attached to doing is the knowledge that comes, perhaps, from being there or from charting data. Being there gives one a kind of assurance that one knows what really happened. Like the computerized readouts of an exercise bicycle, the records of doing, like annals and images, chart effort, repetition, and an objective, technological system of the recording itself, but they do not record intention or meanings. They chart only a presence as a fact. In this sense, the data exhibits an even more authoritative, objective, even totalitarian source than the narrative form of an act. Yet that facticity—that raw data, the physics of pure motion and activity—is nonetheless a crucial dimension of action that provides a reality check against the interpretive judgments of the coroner and the gravedigger alike.

In the absence of will, in other words, Ophelia could very easily be carried away on her song and pure momentum: she is (and is shown in all the paintings) passive to the effects of the water, as the gravedigger suggests: the water comes to her, and she drowns not herself. It does not, therefore, argue an act but an event that is innocent of intentions.

To Perform

Textually speaking, Ophelia never performs her death. Gertrude performs it for her in an eloquent speech. On a stage fraught with so
many bodies at the end, Shakespeare would seem to have no scruples
about keeping deaths offstage, although a drowning might be a difficult death to show on stage. Her death, though, is an absent fact,
given qualities by Gertrude's speech and judgment by the coroner.
Ophelia only appears later as a corpse. But it is primarily through
quality, not an object, that her death occurs as performance, and that
quality distinguishes *to perform* from the other two dimensions of an
act.

     This aspect, however, is a feature of the public nature of perfor-
mance. That is, qualities are not only conceived and done, they are
perceived in public, and executed *for* a public or, simply, another. If
the act-dimension gets values and meanings imposed upon it by the
social context, the performance dimension engages an audience with
sensory qualities in an exchange that can best be called erotic. Clearly
there are overlapping functions in the terms: whatever is performed
will have at some level both the intentionality to be in public and the
actuality of something done. That much intention can be ascribed to
the performer: she is there for an audience. From an intentionalist
perspective, the audience is the telos or reason for the performance,
and in that sense the audience, in return, can judge the performance
as an act, as a way of asserting its power over the performance. But
to receive the performance act means to suspend that assertion of
power and to be more receptively *with* the performer. As Peter
Handke put it in "Offending the Audience," "You are the
topic . . . . You are the center. You are the occasion. You are the reason why."[27] This reason why is not a teleology in an Aristotelian
sense. It is, rather, the occasion of the other, in the Lacanian sense
that it is the other whose presence, akin to the analyst's, provides a
certain demand. While in the area of *to act* the observer is something
like the constructing consciousness, and the act is constructed as an
object of knowledge, in performance the audience is more like a call
for an exchange.

     The performer answers this demand by seductive techniques.
In the taxonomy of act, do, and perform, the performer need not be

communicative, in the sense of communicating meaning. The response to the demand is at an erotic level that takes place in the play of signifiers that do not signify. An extreme example of this can be found in certain songs when the lyrics degenerate, so to speak, into rhythmic sounds, often repeated in a chorus, sounds like do-dah, do-dah, or dit-di-dit-di-dit, or sha-nah-nah. The pleasure, or erotic dimension, of such nonsense comes, in part, from the freedom from meaning, in part from the openness, in part from the rhythm, in part from particularity of the excess.

A similar freedom, openness, rhythm, and particularity can be found in athletic performances. One way to mark the dimension of pleasure is to note the difference between watching an event whose outcome is known and watching it as it is played out. If you know the outcome, watching the football game may be very interesting from a technical point of view, but not much fun. The fun comes from the unknown outcome that requires you be going along with the event, in the sensory play of its signifiers, before it is signified and encorpsed, before the final judgment has been made. Although the intentions of the players are present, although the material constraints are operating, the game generates a rhythm as it goes; its final meaning or score is in suspense; it does not yet designate a winner. Likewise, even the repetition of well-known plays whose story is known gives pleasure to the degree that the performance, first, is *for* the audience, answering a demand of this time and this place and, second, because its qualitative elements are both attached to and free of determinate meanings.

Gertrude's performance of Ophelia's death is *for* the court and for a theater audience. It is a lyrical rhetoric. Aimed *at* the court and the larger audience, it is also a self-contained set piece that seduces by means of its own excesses. Those excesses have force, to be sure. More than describing or giving information, the speech serves to render pathos to the scene of the death, to offer sympathy, to keep Ophelia aligned with sexual images and, intentionally or not, to move Laertes to an exit.

> There is a willow grows askant the brook,
> That shows his hoar leaves in the glassy stream.
> There with fantastic garlands did she make
> Of crowflowers, nettles, daisies, and long purples,

That liberal shepherds give a grosser name,
But our cold maids do dead men's fingers call them.
There on the pendent boughs her crownet weeds
Clamb'ring to hang, an envious sliver broke,
When down her weedy trophies and herself
Fell in the weeping brook. Her clothes spread wide,
And mermaid-like awhile they bore her up,
Which time she chanted snatches of old lauds,
As one incapable of her own distress,
Or like a creature native and indued
Unto that element. But long it could not be
Till that her garments, heavy with their drink,
Pulled the poor wretch from her melodious lay
To muddy death.

                                        (4.7.165–82)

It might be difficult to say why Gertrude spends so long on the list of flowers, why she takes two whole verses for the suggestive digression on those long purples; difficult to know whether she is aware of repeating the long *e* vowels in "weedy" and "weeping." One cannot, that is, necessarily ascribe motive to Gertrude for the rhetoric of the speech: but it does have its effect on Laertes, if not on Claudius or us. As Bert States has said of this speech,

> it is clear that she knows what she is saying, though perhaps not all she is saying; for there is something about the speech in excess of character psychology that makes one wonder about the need for getting so much local etymology into such an urgent report. Of course this could be explained conventionally by the omniscient liberties usually granted to a messenger speech.[28]

My point is that whether one wants to ascribe the rhetoric to Gertrude or to Shakespeare, this speech renders specific qualities to Ophelia's death, qualities that are available to further interpretation and associations but that initially make it concrete, or as concrete as a linguistic medium can render it. It is in terms of those specifics and strategies, the effectiveness of the utterance, that performance may be distinguished in the architecture of the act. The performance turns self-consciously toward the audience to deliver most effectively and efficiently the *sense* of that death. The performance most literally appeals to the senses and sensibilities of its audience, but the appeal is through its rhythm and the feel of its words, not its facts. Gertrude performs Ophelia's death in a lyric style, in keeping with (or helping to create) Ophelia's qualities. Those circumstances are the terrain and the demands created by complex events in the play—Hamlet's rejection, frustrated sexuality, her father's death, Ophelia's previous actions—and by the cultural climate of a theater audience—attitudes toward women, toward suicide, toward poetry. Gertrude's stylization in performance both confirms and creates an audience's perceptions and expectations for Ophelia. Does the Gertrude-actress convey jealously, grief, disgust in her own attitude? Had she entered and said only, "The girl, my lord, is dead," or if she showed disgust, Ophelia might be re-created or converted into something more nasty, brutish, and short than that which her own lyrical madness has already shown. Both versions would be performances, but performances in very different styles, with very different effects. Hearing Gertrude's speech, one does not necessarily analyze its rhetoric but succumbs to it. Hence its relation with the pleasure of the senses.

From Gertrude's speech and the reaction of Claudius, Hamlet, and Laertes to the news, we take it for granted that Ophelia went through certain motions and died. The speech, that is, covers an event that is not staged. A director can, of course, choose to stage a scene for Ophelia. My point, however, in using this example for performance is to indicate how performance might be understood as standing in for or covering for an absent, unstaged act, which is a "thing of nothing." Death in particular can never be enacted or represented except as a performance because it is the ultimate "other" for life. Yet the reality of death, of nothingness, stands behind or within performance, guaranteeing only the truth of its own otherness and the absence of a substantive thing. Like Lacan's "veiled Phallus,"[29] but without the attachment to the gendered, sexual image, Gertrude's performance of Ophelia's death conceals its own lack of attachment to what it signifies, for it signifies an unrepresentable absence. Performance is unmoored; like "do-dah" lyrics, it is detached from a signified even in the process of signifying. It neither gives the act a name and a form nor, exactly, materializes it, though names, forms, and matter enter into performance. On the one hand, then, its lack of substance makes it a somewhat uncanny dimension of action;

on the other hand, its very effectiveness—its capacity to move an audience to tears or revenge—makes it a highly social dimension. Performance occurs on surfaces, as though it had neither depth or delay. Like the mythical figure of Hermes, performance functions in between, like a go-between; it is everywhere and nowhere. Recalling Wittgenstein's question about the subtraction between "my arm goes up" and "I raise my arm," I would point to the subtraction itself as a possible site for performance. Instead of saying that the remainder is an intention, as above, the leftover or excess could instead be called performance.

The relation of actor to character is another case in point. Character is a textual function that is performed by an actor, but the substance of a character is absent except as a linguistic construct. The textual Ophelia is a system of constraints: what she says, what is said about her, what consequences her presence has in the constellation of other characters. The performance of Ophelia, however, is a qualitative manifestation not only of those constraints but also of the particularity of the actress who performs her and the choices made onstage. Is it Claire Bloom or Ellen Terry in performance? Does she overhear Hamlet's "To be or not to be" or enter after? Is she furious in her madness or just dotty? Is she dignified or doting? The differences are crucial to the performance. The Hamlet of Olivier will not be identical to the Hamlet of Richard Burton or Mel Gibson. This is an obvious enough assertion, but it has important implications for what performance is. For the actual appearance of Bloom or Olivier or Burton functions like a rhetoric of excess. That is, their particularity is part of what helps to persuade an audience not only of the reality of the character but also of that reality's qualities. That particularity is in excess of any idea of an essential character named Hamlet, but the excess itself is vital to the seduction of the audience. Directors casting the parts of the play know how crucial the look of a character is: apart from acting skill, apart from the transformative possibilities in costume and makeup, a specific actor brings specific qualities to a role, qualities that will engage in persuading an audience through an appeal to the senses and not, initially, to an idea.

The actress performing Ophelia carries with her a bodily, psychological, and social history that she cannot avoid bringing along. The performer stands directly in the face and presence of the audience, with a combination of the conscious choices and the baggage of both bodily presence and unconscious determinants, all of which are manifest in externals. How that presence signifies to an audience is historically bound to conceptions of both real persons and conventions of theatricality. The actress herself is already a signified body as well as a performer who chooses to signify. The performer is a function in this way, more than an object. And its function is to play with and for an audience.

As the third term in the gravediggers anatomy, *to perform* is both medial, standing between act and do, and formative, at the public edge where the act opens into a sensory and social world where it is subject to immediate interpretation and judgment. It is neither part of the sedimentation of the narrative act, which traverses past and future in a portable form, nor of the present tense of the body. It serves both, however, in phenomenological terms, by breaking up the false dichotomy between the purely conceptual and the purely physical. The dichotomy is false because it limits the conceptual to a purely abstract form of knowledge and the physical to the world of objects, as though those objects were not also inscribed with signification.[30]

The narrative act is not an abstraction, but it is something like Ophelia's corpse. It is portable but lifeless. Performance, particularly in enactment, accomplishes a revival of the corpse not simply as a purely physical doing, but as a stylization of behavior that has cultural significations. Pleasure, that is, cannot be free of culture. Yet the significations are not named, as they are in *act*, but are felt. Rather than the sense of objectivity in the actual that *to do* emphasizes, *to perform* makes the actual appear in the shifting middle ground, in between what Natalie Crohn Schmitt calls "actors and onlookers," between the discursive and the material, between the imaginary and the real. The behavior and gestures of performer take their significance from a field of cultural codes that they can either reinforce or disrupt. The performative gesture circulates those codes between an a priori field and the present. This is how the performance of an old play like *Hamlet* can constantly adjust to contemporary cultural values, can alter prior conceptions of *Hamlet* and in turn offer new possibilities for the perception of *Hamlet*. The performance furthermore veils the absence of a substantive *Hamlet*. That stylization is to a large degree the function of performance as the strategic response to the conditions of its audience and its demands to be seduced. Yet it is a function—or what Lacan calls an algorithm—only. It is an operation without an object. Identical to neither the messenger nor the message, performance nonetheless occurs *for* and in the immediate context of an other. If Hamlet appears on roller skates, he is not only going to break up conventional ideas about how Hamlet usually moves, he also adds a sensory quality of movement to the quality of character. The performance on roller skates has little to do with a character of weak intentions or will and everything to do with how Hamlet plays with the audience. Of course, if *Hamlet* were always played on roller skates, the convention itself would atrophy the seductive exchange—habit, as Beckett said, being the great deadener.

As an example, Josette Féral has pointed out how the function of performance art in the 1970s and 1980s has gradually been converted into a genre. The functional purposes she lists—to deny representation in favor of a real presence, to oppose commercial values in art, to privilege process over product, to join art with life, and to refuse any identification that would contribute to catharsis—have been converted, she claims, into a form rather than a function. It is a form that has identifiable messages and signification, values efficiency in the use of its media, and conveys ideas about reality and art.[31] More than a set of meanings, however, I think it would be possible to say that the performance art of the period has become an identifiable *style*. The look of performance art has become customary. It has become a genre less, perhaps, because of its content than because it became a recognizable style of behavior. What is more, however, it could not be restyled in the way that *Hamlet* can be because part of its look, so to speak, was its unrepeatability. While the record of performance art is more archival than analytic, the archives tell of deeds done. The more analysis is applied to performance art, the more performance art becomes a generic category rather than a performative function.

In a similar way all performance styles evolve into generic categories as they become customary. One can notice that evolution at the point at which the style can be parodied. When an attitude becomes subject to parody, one could say that its stylistic consistencies have coalesced into a recognizable system of attitudes. Certainly in literary history this has not been the only way of describing genres, and major arguments have raged over whether the single day that a tragedy should take is eight, twelve, or twenty-four hours. For my purposes, however, genres locate habits of performance behavior. But almost at the same moment a generality appears, actual performances begin to resist and attempt alternative styles in order to break generic categories: they become mixed and combinatory. The alternatives, however, develop habits that in turn become categorical. Polonius's famous list catalogs the absurdity and the inevitability of the turn from an attitude to a genre. "Tragedy, comedy, history, pastoral, pastoral-comical, historical-pastoral, tragical-historical, tragical-comical-historical-pastoral." Styles, like sorrows, don't necessarily come in single spies, but in battalions. Likewise, the particular performance of a given text makes stylistic adjustments to that text that identify a given moment in theatrical history as much if not more than the style of the literary work. Peter Hall's *Midsummer Night's Dream*, once an up-to-the-minute stylization of that play as a hippie love fest, now seems hopelessly dated and looks almost like a self-parody.

The value of performance as opposed to action is precisely that it is an indicator of its historical moment. Its function is total thisness of here and now, like doing. Unlike doing, however, it is necessarily defined as a relation. Performance is thus the social, political, or relational dimension of action in the domain of desire. It is where *to act* returns to a social context through *to do*. Like *to act*, it is mediated through signs, norms, and symbols. Performance is rather more like an utterance than the grammatical system of an intentional act. Performance in this sense is an exteriority, a surface, a concrete perception of material features that can be seen in the difference, say, between Olivier's face and Mel Gibson's. In this sense, performance is style that actualizes the structure of an act.[32] Yet, like Roland Barthes's definition of "the third meaning," my sense of performance "exceeds meaning without, however, coming down to the obstinacy in presence shown by any human body."[33]

Performance could be defined as a rhetorical posture that seeks maximum effectiveness, hence its association with sophistry as a triumph of style over substance. When attitude eclipses intention, performance is all surface. One of Robert Wilson's paradigmatic performers, for example, is Ethel Merman, whom he describes as "being right there in the center of the music, sockin' it to 'em." As opposed to imitating some other identity, or pretending to some role, Ethel Merman was less a person (as in *agent*) than a summation of attitude, but an attitude of performing itself, something close to pure style. Ethel Merman is not a character, she is a self-defining attitude that is virtually tautological; she thus becomes a category in herself.

Perform is also an empty term, like do. But unlike doing, the notion performing sustains a sense of completing, not, again, in a teleological sense but in the sense of bringing into being in a perceptible manner. Grammar, again, can falsify the sense of performance, as in the phrase, "the performance *of* an action." We speak in terms that suggest performance is a kind of transference or translation of some other thing, as though performance has a direct object: whether it is a hostess performing a role, an actress performing a character, a comic performing a joke, an athlete performing skills, a professor performing thoughts. But what does it mean, for example, when one says a car performs? It is not that the car is performing its carness but that it is some sense working to a capacity, and in fulfilling that capacity in a particular manner. The Jaguar has a style different from a Honda, and it is easy to turn that style into a conceptual essence of Jaguarness. But because performance is an exteriority, like doing, the performance of the car is not *of* an essence. To say the car performs is to answer the question of how it is working; that is, it is a mannerly description that joins up the car's style with an idea of substance.

Judgments of performance are therefore aesthetic judgments relating to pleasure. This in part has to do with an assessment of the risks involved: it was an exciting or boring football match, engaging or tedious opera, skillful or amateur circus, dangerous or safe high-wire act, interesting or dull actor. There is a commonplace that the most dangerous actors are the most interesting to watch. We watch with more interest the people who are seductive. They may seem to threaten to break out of their character, their script, their role; they are answering our demands for pleasure, and we admire their skill tested against difficult odds. And playwrights give characters their moments of seduction, which tend to be high points in a text. Such is the source of admiration for moments such as Marc Antony's speech to the Romans, Iago's insinuations to Othello, or Richard III's wooing of Anne. Within and without those plays, the audience is hostile: it has been persuaded by Brutus's justification for Caesar's murder; it is devoted to Desdemona; it mourns with Anne for a dead husband. The rhetorical skills of Antony, Iago, or Richard have less to do with logical argument than the ways in which they style their appeals. The audience ends by admiring not the sincerity but the technique that allowed them to overcome apparently insurmountable difficulties, and both audiences finally consent. If performance is limited by the decorum of circumstances, its pleasurable danger is nonetheless in the fact that the performer can overcome those limits and succeed in the nonsignifying, erotic dimension in between meaning and matter.

Performance, the libidinal dimension in action, situates an erotic exchange of the pleasure in playing for, with, in, and among others and asks its audience to play along. When Richard is clearly having so much fun in his wooing, it requires a very surly disposition to resist. When one speaks or writes of performance, language tends to become hysterical, "deictic," as Barthes said of the pleasure of the text.[34] Performance need not be fathomed, it need only be there for us and our senses. When performance art is theorized or analyzed, however important that may be, it becomes a corpse. I do not want to fathom performance because I don't want to kill it: it is too identical to direct experience. Ideas, structures, intents, texts may be performed and mediated through the senses, but in the primacy of performance, pleasure is primary.

Defined by these differences, "to act, to do, and to perform" might usefully outline the most general range of perspectives on action. It encompasses the intentional, the physical, and the pleasurable; the cognitive, the rhetorical, and the formal,[35] all depending on the position of an onlooker in a culture. Indeed, the gravedigging clown gives the most general formulation by his use of infinitive, the part of speech that is not attached to persons or tense, time or agents. It is a formula that appeals to universals by its detachment from specific cases.

The infinitive also serves to coalesce the functions of noun and verb. That is, it disintegrates the differences between time and objects, such that objects are not exclusively things in temporal space. Rather, time itself is part of the constitution of the object. In breaking up the attachment of an act to a person predicate, by which the person is constituted prior to an act, the infinitive asserts a paradoxical sense of the act as both free of and bound to past and future, in the way that things that are present bear their own pasts and futures.

Actions sustain that temporality through memory, attention, and anticipation. Action, in this sense, is a version of Augustine's notion of time, a threefold present that accounts for the experience of time as both a present and as duration through pasts and futures. It likewise presents a similar aporia between the experience and the conceptualization. In this sense, the experience of time, like the experience of action, can most accurately be described in language by the empty form of the infinitive, since any particularity in description turns the experience into an object: it breaks up experience into its constituent, analytic, observable, and comprehensible parts that are no longer identical to how things happen.

The joining of the noun and verb in many ways is as empty as the self-defining analytic of act, do, and perform. That is, it points out how conceptualization requires a rupture in the phenomenon of action. Like Heidegger's habit of making tautological sentences such as "the world worlds," the infinitive announces a combined sense of facticity, of object, of temporality, and of exchange. It uses a grammatical and syntactic strategy to invoke a recognition of what could be called a *pregrammatic* condition. That is, it impossible to think without the analytic tools of grammar, but such analysis leads away from the sense of experiential totality. The consciousness formed in language is separate from its object, perhaps, but it attempts, in the kind of language that Heidegger uses, to speak the thought that thinks about itself. The question is the degree to which a concept is identical to that which it conceives, and the degree to which the unthought escapes concept. The problem is that the most accurate representation of the unity of being is an almost unintelligible tautology, such as "the world worlds" or "appropriation appropriates." On the other hand, the use of two parts of speech in such formulas, suggests that action, like time or being, is not exclusively a unity but is already composed of ruptures and discontinuities.

But this is exactly the usefulness of drama in the theater as the mode for understanding action. For in the theater, the observing, temporal consciousness is the audience. It is both separate from the action and participating in it; observing action, the audience is also the condition for it. For it does not merely observe action as an object, it suffers the action as a whole. There is more to Ophelia than can be named by *suicide* or any other single noun. The gravedigger's humor underlines the radical difference between analytic proof and experience. The audience knows more about Ophelia than can be named because it suffers along through the play, oscillating between naming her act and undergoing it. If philosophy asks for the name of the act, drama, as a temporal mode, asks for undergoing or suffering a process. The difference is not so much the relative truth-value of philosophy versus that of drama as the kind and quality of the knowledge rendered: to know the logic is not to know the suffering.

But the question remains, where is Ophelia in all this generality? In part, this is a question of how one understands character and the relation between action and identity: as a representation of human agency with motives and intentions; as a product of textual constraints and ideological systems; or as an embodied appeal and a figured presence. A full description of Ophelia, as of any other character, would need to take each of these possibilities into account or at least recognize what perspectives are suppressed in the account. For Ophelia, like characters in general, not only resides in the spaces between these perspectives, she in some sense identifies those spaces. Her death in particular exhibits the way that action is represented simultaneously as a representation (the corpse, a completed identity), a product of a textual system (what she says and what is said of her), and a rhetorical quality that conceals her absence (in Gertrude's speech as well as in the actress portraying her). Any one perspective on Ophelia will more than likely throw the sight back at the observer and show less of her as an object and more of the interests and perspectives of the onlooker. Together, the representation, the products, and the rhetoric identify the subject *en procès*, as Kristeva put it: a subject on trial through process, who appears not as an object but as a social relation, at once present, encorpsed, anticipated, and remembered.

For all his abstraction, and the designation of the phenomenon of action, however, the clown does not leave Ophelia without some specific valuation. The final irony in his explanation of Ophelia's death is in how the coroner found—that is, decided—it was not a suicide. The coroner himself is absent from *Hamlet* except as a discursive judgment. His absence suggests the ironic awareness that judgments of an act are made at a remove, by a cultural apparatus. The judgment finally is based on class: "If this had not been a gentlewoman, she should have been buried out o' Christian burial" (5.1.21–23). For finally, the gravedigger is a cultural materialist, whose ironic view of action and of law is that all is not equal under the sun and under the inquest of the coroner. The exercise in determining the nature of her action is then just that—an exercise whose consequence is determined by the facts of Ophelia's place in the world of *Hamlet* as a gentlewoman. The gravedigger recognizes that pronouncements by the law are finally determined by the context of class, when the reality of the act escapes any final determination.

The relation of the terms is more usefully understood, I think, as a recursive system. Each aspect participates with the others in a kind of chaotic feedback loop that generates a virtually infinite number of possible forms for understanding action. The result is a history of dramatic literature and theater whose differences demonstrate the complex interaction between the act as the dimension of intentionality and motive, the deed as the objectified product of systems, and the performance as a libidinal exchange. A history of dramatic literature and criticism might well examine not a chronology but the degree to which any given work emphasizes the ethical agent-act relation, the impersonal, formal, and physical, or the rhetorical, sensory, and pleasurable. The interplay of these perspectives leads to an assessment not of the act alone but of the cultural milieu in which they arose and in which they are replayed. The model suggests that to understand an act is itself a recursive act that implicates not only agents but the cultural arena in which an action is perceived.

The social dimension will tend to aim toward the act in the sense that public meaning consistently seeks stability and the certainties of retrospection, as opposed to the prospects of further rippling and open-ended play and pleasure. In an act of interpretation of meaning, that is, the performative dimension will tend to return toward the name of an act. The name, in turn, will on the one hand identify both subject and act, but *as* a name it will inhibit or resist material activity. The actuality of *doing* will unname the act, taking it out of a language and into matter. But that material dimension threatens to make the act into noise and the subject into something that is wholly an object.

The categories, however, do not progress or develop to some final point. Performance is not a result but rather a beginning. Yet the doing of any given performance will create its own past and become available to the reification, narration, and textuality of the act. Drama, the act, the subject, and time, rather than being preexisting, substantive categories can be recognized as *effects* that acquire a substantive status only in the requirements of a grammar. The subject is a signifying and signified effect. It is the product of what could be called temporal pressures, but because they are temporal, the subject, like the act, is open and incomplete: never finally produced.

Chapter 2

To Act: "Did That Never Happen to You?"

At the opening of *Waiting for Godot,* Estragon is trying to take off his boot. As directed in the text by Beckett, he pulls at it with both hands, gives up, rests, tries again. After the initial exchanges between Didi and Gogo, Vladimir eventually asks, "What are you doing?" Estragon replies, "Taking off my boot. Did that never happen to you?"[1] When this line is played on stage, the odd rhetoric of the statement is usually overshadowed by the energetic suffering of Estragon's attempts to remove his boot. His activity overwhelms the implications, so in performance the description of the act tends to get lost in the evidence of his struggle.

There are, however, many possible responses to Vladimir's question. Estragon might have said, "I'm waiting for you," or "I'm playing with my feet," or "I'm losing hope," or "I'm recovering from last night's beating." Whatever he says, that is, clearly indicates a specific framing from a field of all possible but still true responses—or at least all those that would conform to appearances. By saying, "I'm taking off my boot," Estragon has directed attention to a specific sense of his intention, activity, and purpose.

But most fundamentally Estragon has added language to his being there and doing something in such a way that one might assume that taking off his boot is all he is doing and all he could be doing. The other possible descriptions of his intent, desire, or purpose are excluded, at least from our attention. But the fact of such exclusions points out how thoroughly language both defines and constitutes the identity of the act. By attributing an intention to the activity, Estragon has defined his act *as* an act and he has limited its frame by his language. Other statements that might conform to the material or visible activities remain unidentified. Another way of saying this is that the semiotic dimension of his action—what he signifies it to be—approaches but does not consume the tautological dimension of his activity—the fact of his being there and doing—nor does it contain all the other possible descriptions that remain beyond or in excess of the particular description, "I'm taking off my boot." Through the language of intention Estragon represents the act as a re-presentation. But such representation is not just a double or addendum or attachment of language to a series of motions: it is an act of creation of an identity.

As outlined in the last chapter, the attribution of motive or intention is the basis for the distinction of *act* as opposed to *activity* in philosophy since Aristotle.[2] What is rarely examined is how motive or intention is bound less to "fact" than to language and how language constitutes acts by framing them, in the same way that Estragon identified his act by selecting one possible description among others. Action is a discursive phenomenon to a significant degree, bound to the selective fictions and semiotic possibilities of language. It is thus also constructed grammatically to structure relations between subjects and acts. Grammar both constructs and constrains the understanding of action, determining what can and cannot be represented as action in contrast to activity or motion.

Drama coaches, directors, and teachers since Stanislavski have tended to assume this dimension of action as the basis of acting, without necessarily recognizing it as a discursive form. In acting classes, one often hears, "What does the character *want* here?" in an attempt to help the actor to define and activate a motive. The question became so common that it provided a basis for the parody of American method acting, when actors might refuse to act until they had "found" their motivation, as though it had been lost somewhere. The usefulness of such a question, pragmatically speaking, is that it often gives an actor a quality of erotic energy that enlivens a flat performance. It activates a kind of desire in a performer. The parodic potential of the question, to my mind, is that the object of desire or intention is arbitrary. What matters is not the object of intent, and it is not the rational volition that matters but a sense of force. Desire or erotic energy can be activated by an idea of anything from a wish to eat the chocolate cake to a desire to murder the king. What the acting teacher or director is trying to elicit is a performance energy, but she disguises the point in terms of volition. This can be a useful ruse, since the actor needs specificity. But it leads to an almost infinite regress of motivation and forces the actor to initiate an action, to be a self-starting cause for action. Hence the parody of actors who stay offstage indefinitely, looking for the lost motive instead of *doing* something. My point is simply to indicate how the severe bracketing of action as a goal-directed, intentionalist form shows up in pragmatic circumstances and reinforces the notion that an agent is prior to or behind an act rather than in it.

If the normative identity of action is based upon a volitional subject, however, Estragon goes on to indicate how volition also puts an agent in a passive position. In the following discussion I hope to indicate how the volitional structure serves the traditional sense of action and mimesis, whose fullest expression has been tragic form, in which active and passive become identical, if paradoxical, positions. But I also want to suggest the limitations of such completeness, since volition alone is not a sufficient account for action.

First the paradox. After Estragon tells Vladimir that he is taking off his boot, he counters with a question of his own: "Did that never happen to you?" One might reasonably ask, "did *what* never happen to you?" What does he mean? The question is elliptical, to be sure, but it is also revealing because it articulates a repositioning of his own agency from active to passive. In terms of the Aristotelian distinction between voluntary and involuntary, the juxtaposition of statements is contradictory and absurd. How is it possible for taking off his boot to be something that happens *to* him? Taking off the boot may happen to the boot, but how is it something that happens to Estragon? The universe may rebound on Oedipus for asking too many questions, but can a boot be so perverse? The action should appear to be something he is responsible for, something for which he can be held accountable for doing. Recall that the volitional structure asserts a relation between intentions and goals, linear time and the subject; it further marks off past and future, beginning and end.[3] Volition and narrative time go hand in hand. Volition passes into plot because it already is a plotted association of acts and agents. The conceptual network, in Ricoeur's terms, describes the coherence of beginnings and ends, offering the possibility of closure, completion and identity. The name frees the act from its inchoate present and gives it identity. But in the process the act is converted into a *thing* like a table or a refrigerator. At the same time, it becomes inextricable from the agent, and the agent conforms to the act, as in the line from *Macbeth:* "To know the deed, 'twere best not know myself." Kenneth Burke provides an example of how the active and passive combine to create a personal identity for the agent:

> Once one has jumped over a cliff, for instance, he can let events take care of themselves, confident in the knowledge that he will continue to maintain and intensify his character as one-who-has-jumped-over-a-cliff.[4]

Once Estragon takes off his boot, similarly, he can be confident (and appalled) that he will continue to be one-who-has-taken-off-his-boot. The correlation of the nameable act with the written text, or work, is obvious. Volition provides the identity that converts into the notion of plot and character. The character that aims toward a goal is also one that is created by that goal.[5] If a narrative structure anticipates the retrospect that an end point provides, Estragon and Burke indicate that the retrospect tied to the assertion. In doing something, Estragon is being done. That is, he is making a self as he appears to be doing other things.[6] It is as though no matter what he does, or what he says he is doing, he cannot avoid making a plot, creating a past, accumulating an identity, making an act to which he is passive.[7] At this extreme, Vladimir and Estragon are wholly victimized by time itself, and, at this extreme, they are wholly modernist figures. In "The Sociology of Modern Drama," Lukács notes:

> Hebbel was the first to recognize that the difference between action and suffering is not quite so profound as the words suggest; that every suffering is really an action directed from within, and every action which is directed against destiny assumes the form of suffering. Man grows dramatic by virtue of the intensity of his will. . . . The heroes of the new drama . . . are more passive than active; they are acted upon more than they act for themselves; they defend rather than attack; their heroism is mostly a heroism of anguish, of despair, not one of bold aggressiveness.[8]

Now, if all interest in Estragon, Vladimir, Pozzo, and Lucky lay in what they did in terms of volitional acts, the play might have sunk into the obscurity its early critics anticipated. For their trivial games—eating carrots, insulting, asking questions, taking off boots or hats—

do in themselves hardly seem worthy of any attention. The retrospect on such activities does not really add up to any other name than waiting. But it is just because of the waiting that one might say that this play does not trace a development from volition to its retrospective narrative, from active to passive, but demonstrates their simultaneity, in the same way that Estragon's line, "I'm taking off my boot. Did that never happen to you?" suggests a coalescence of active and passive. Such simultaneity prevents the action of the play from being summed up in narrative closure.

Anthony Kenny distinguishes between activity verbs that cover actions that endure, go on, last, or persist and performance verbs that concern actions that take time and come to a definite end: "Only . . . performance verbs have a true passive voice. In common speech we distinguish between things which we do, and things which happen to us."[9] The distinction is important for pointing out a difference between those actions that have an end point and those that have endurance. "We may ask how long it took to paint a door blue, but not how long it took the door to be blue," says Kenny.[10]

Waiting, in this play particularly, is something that the characters do—something that takes time and involves volition. But it is also something like a state, as in Kenny's example of the door being blue. The state of being—waiting—conditions the action and also comprises the action. Waiting does have an end: the actual end of the play and the analogous end of a life span. And although their waiting is to some measure a volitional act, it is also completely dependent upon something outside itself to determine the end of waiting. One waits *for* the end, or *for* Godot. No volitional act other than suicide can bring about the end, so apart from suicide, waiting becomes condition in which the agent is passive in relation to the end. The time before the end is to-be-endured. Duration, however, is comprised of volitional activities: the relationship is circular. Godot, however, indicates the imaginary nature of an end and a name. The name of "Godot" is only a rationale, never a concrete reality.

There is an analogy here in the relationship between performances and texts. The text, made up of dialogue and directions, tends to authorize performance acts. Although the text is not precisely made of action, action is nonetheless textual. The text may justify, rationalize, outline, or indicate: but action cannot be itself in name only; it must be enacted. For Didi and Gogo, the absence of

Godot leads to an *effect* of their having to create their own ends, like performers improvising. They say, "Nothing to be done." And that is to say, there is nothing demanded of them; nothing preceding them; they can anticipate no future retrospect upon the present; there is nothing imposing its will, identity, or meaning upon them, not even their own future selves or a text. This is a fiction, of course, given the meticulous detail that is Beckett's textual habit. He leaves less room for volitional or improvisatory acts on the part of his actors than almost any other playwright. But it is perhaps just because of that detail that he is able to represent the phenomenon of *action* so precisely. That is, action appears not in terms of a name that identifies intention, but as a fact, devoid of a justifying end point.

The stage figures in *Godot* are seen to struggle between the name and the behavior itself. And that name is clearly shown, by its absence, to be an imaginary projection. Action, that is, occurs precisely in between, as a fact, but resting neither in its name nor in behavior alone. The volition of the actor is extraneous to the simultaneous active-passive position of the character-figures. The action is textual not because it is written but because it does *not* come to rest in either a name or an end. Particularly in Beckett's plays after *Not I*, speech, as action, is something that happens to the stage figures, something that emerges autonomously from their mouths. Bruce Wilshire describes this perception of the phenomenon in the tradition of Vico's *Scienza nuova*, one of Beckett's few books, as "an account of the evolution of the experience of the world in which the true and the made, *verum* and *factum*, are convertible."[11]

The "canters and chronicles" by which Didi and Gogo pass the time, then, both make the time of the play and fill the time. This is a conventional point in the critical literature on *Godot*. But if this play in particular foregrounds the sensation of what it feels like when action is both active and passive, it also exposes the condition of Vladimir and Estragon's predicament, of emplotment at large, and of plotted characters in general. More precisely, it uncovers the simultaneity of the given and the created. For the same grammar of action that combines active and passive undermines the sense of action as a substantive noun and suggests that endings are not singular end points; it subverts the notion of a subject as a source; it questions the authority of the text as the cause of dramatic acts.

In suffering the inescapability of duration Vladimir and Estragon are, from one perspective, classical heroes who bear duration as destiny. The suffering of classical tragic heroes is not that they "feel bad" about things. The tragic suffering of Didi and Gogo is specifically related to a form of action in which suffering takes on its more archaic meaning in the sense of experiencing or letting something happen.[12] To suffer is to bear the weight of experience—a weight that deforms and defines the particularity of an identity. Vladimir and Estragon suffer the weight of duration that identifies them and makes them tragic as well as modernist heroes. In *Proust*, Beckett uses the active/passive construction in regard to time:

> There is no escape from the hours and the days. Neither from to-morrow nor from yesterday. There is no escape from yesterday because yesterday has deformed us, or been deformed by us. The mood is of no importance. Deformation has taken place.[13]

Deforming and deformation are simultaneous in Beckett's view. And Estragon's statement is also suggesting that *every* present act of assertion is on a temporal verge of its own past and is indeed creating its own past as it goes. Although the end is usually understood as the end of the play or the conclusion of the plot, or the end of a life, one can also see each present moment as an end. As Didi and Gogo engage in their play and diversion that would seem to resist the end of the play itself, they are also creating ends all along. If the doing is in the active indicative, present tense, the done represents the combination of death and identity in the form of a fact, which is made at every moment. The corpse of the act—the corpse that *is* the act—is the name and identity that narrative would confer only after the end or by anticipating that end. But from Estragon's statement, one might consider that such a name and identification does not come simply at the end of the action, or in anticipation of the end; it is carried along with the action, at every moment, in the identity of Estragon.

The name that inhabits action all along, indicating to whom it belongs, is something like inert matter, but matter that situates an identity for the act, as for example, *revenge* inhabits Hamlet through all his activities or *waiting* inhabits every activity of Didi and Gogo. The identity, however, is partial: it does not encompass all possible identifications or the actuality of practices. The action of the play and its characters can neither escape the name of Godot or the identity the name represents, nor can they come to rest in the name, assured that acting and identity are coextensive.

Apart from its reflection of Aristotelian coherence and totality, that is, the grammatic conflation of active and passive announces some elements in the nature of action that are grammatically incoherent but phenomenally actual. The correlation of the active and passive to the phenomenon of dramatic action is a significant way of demonstrating how drama dissolves the actual differences between the conceptual, nominative form of the act and the practice of an act yet also keeps them distinctive. In practice, that is, the structure of action as a substantive thing having attributes turns out to be only a conceptual paradox, not a real one. For example, there is a commonsense habit to speak of the "representation of character" or to discuss the "performance of a text." Character or text stands, however interestingly or problematically, as the stable object from which the representation or the performance derives, such that the representation or performance is subordinate to the larger concept that would seem to be a precondition for the event of representation or performance.

This is the grammatical basis for the concept that a subject resides behind or prior to an action, which is the commonsense notion of *mimesis* or imitation. So character or text would be a subject that is given attributes or qualities by its representation or performance. Or, put another way, a subject would derive qualities from its actions.[14] The paradox for the theatrical character is that enactment appears to depend on a previously existing character constituted by a text. Yet it is difficult to say whether the actor is passive to the written character or the written character is passive to the actor. If Estragon is useful, however, he may be suggesting that the choice between those alternatives is a false one.

Any alternative concept of the relation between subject and attributes is difficult to formulate because the grammar creates the perception of a difference. The following quotation from Nietzsche's *Genealogy of Morals* makes it clear that the perception is a linguistic one. And while one might assume that if it can be said, there must be something behind the saying, any kind of nonsense poem like "Jabberwocky" would suggest that language can easily show something where there is nothing to be seen.[15]

> For just as the popular mind separates the lightning from its flash
> and takes the latter for an *action*, for the operation of a subject
> called lightning, so popular morality also separates strength from
> expressions of strength, as if there were a neutral substratum
> behind the strong man, which was *free* to express strength or not
> to do so. But there is no such substratum; there is no "being"
> behind doing, effecting, becoming; "the doer" is merely a fiction
> added to the deed—the deed is everything.[16]

If lightning is the subject and flash is an action, one would have to
imagine some kind of lightning that does not flash or that has some
other action in order to make the statement meaningful or useful.
This is not to imply that a text sitting on the shelf is the same thing
as a performance, or that lightning cannot strike as well as flash. The
differences are rhetorical, however. But, to speak as though a performance were simply derivative *of* a text that is sitting on a shelf is
equivalent to assuming that there is lightning somewhere apart from
its flash. The text is *other* than performance but is not necessarily the
source, cause, subject, or *maker* of performance. In other words, in
addition to Aristotelian implications and the possibility of constructing a notion of totality out of its formulation, Estragon is in fact
linguistically disintegrating the false assumptions within the substan-
tive/attributive grammar. He is saying something about plotted characters in an Aristotelian sense, to be sure. But at the same time, he
is indicating how the subject/predicate, active indicative grammar of
conventional mimesis is radically altered by the phenomenon itself.
And the collapse of the active/passive is a linguistic means of approaching the phenomenon.

The phenomenon of the stage, that is, unsettles the Aristotelian
grammar of plot and the substantive notion of action. In his commen-
tary on the *Genealogy of Morals*, Michel Haar writes:

> All psychological categories (the ego, the individual, the person)
> derive from the illusion of substantial identity. But this illusion
> goes back basically to a superstition that deceives not only com-
> mon sense but also philosophers—namely, the belief in language
> and, more precisely, in the truth of grammatical categories. It
> was grammar (the structure of subject and predicate) that in-

spired Descartes' certainty that "I" is the subject of "think," whereas it is rather the thoughts that come to "me": at bottom, faith in grammar simply conveys the will to be the "cause" of one's thoughts.[17]

How is it possible to decide, finally, whether Estragon's line is simply replicating a narrative coherence that is death directed, retrospective, representational, and repetitive (as Brooks describes narrative) or whether is it radically disruptive, pointing to a more timeless, chaotic present of theatrical enactment? Perhaps the combination also points to some aspects of action that are both contradictory and simultaneous. As a medium that is constituted by action, drama may well indicate how action is always already a representation. That is to say that the dramatic act does not duplicate some removed, imaginary act, because an act itself is already a representation or construction culled from the realm of all possible descriptions. And no matter what the description of a volitional act may be, the act is simultaneously a fact-in-the-making. This is part of the impossibility of accurately separating the representation of an act from the act of representation. The sense of a representation *of* character or *of* an act is instituted grammatically, separating one from the other in both time (character as preceding) and space (character as elsewhere). In fact, however, the act and character are simultaneous to the representation. While the linguistic formula, as in the flash *of* lightning, the performance *of* a text, or the representation *of* character, is a formula to be wary of and to distrust, this does not mean that the flash, lightning, performance, text, or character are identical: language itself has given them their separate identities. But to assume then that those identities are also natural facts or truths is to assume that language itself is truth. It can be, in fact, useful to distinguish active, volitional formulations from the passive. But by recognizing how action is constituted not only by its name but also by time, in, for example, the present participle of "I'm taking off my boot," we can account for the simultaneity of the name and the event. Temporality constitutes action yet it also creates the apparent paradox of dramatic figures on stage who are moving forward through time while they are also in some sense resting there as already made things.

Estragon's statement is a verbal formulation, then, of the play itself. The simultaneity of active and passive is what gives the dramatic text its status as an artifact; it is also how the dramatic text is an event—like the flash of lightning that is lightning itself. The name and identity are indeed aspects of action, but the nominative is a dimension that conceals both temporal development and temporal immediacy. Even while Estragon, Vladimir, Pozzo, and Lucky are turning themselves into an artifact, or a done deed, their suffering and their exertions undermine the sense of artifact. By his statement, he has altered the notion of a substantive subject and act and converted it to a *textual* subject that develops over time by games, delays, and plays with meanings. This does not mean that the subject is a text, but that it is rather something that is continuously resisting its own completion as a work. Speech is the negotiable element as it manipulates responses to the question, "What are you doing?"

The name of the intent, that is, is negotiable, but those negotiations tend to destabilize the subject. For example, Estragon's speech about his intention might in fact be radically at odds with appearances. What he is doing might not conform to what he says he is intending. It might be possible, as Brecht liked to do, to contradict his character's words, make them ironic. Or, in the visible field of the theater, it could be shown that "taking off my boot" is identical to waiting, suffering, playing. The defining characteristic of *act* as that to which intention can be assigned, then, is complicated and disordered by the very kinesis or pure motion from which the act is supposedly differentiated. Thus, rather than a subject being the origin for the act, a subject could be said to be that which appears in the difference between the articulation and the fact, between the practice and the fiction. The simultaneity of activity and performance verbs show how *Waiting for Godot* (and certainly other Beckett plays) uses dramatic action to reveal action. It represents the collapse of plotted time (the narrative act) into experiential time. The characters are both objects on view and subjects in process who speak from a place of disconformity between experience and what is possible to say. Experience is in a continual present tense; the name of the act can endure past the present. Speaking, however, occurs from the position of a subject in between that escapes from the totalizing aspect of active/ passive.

Wittgenstein's question, quoted in the previous chapter, ("What is left over if I subtract the fact that my arm goes up from the fact that I raise my arm?") is again apt.[18] The leftover, it would seem, is will or intent. The idea that there can be such a subtraction at all points up the possibility of a fracture in the simultaneity of active and passive, a fracture in the constitution of an act from which a speaking self emerges. The subtraction furthermore raises the question of whether or how a negative space can occur in action as well as in language. It also offers an important way for looking at the possibilities for a negative subject, a possibility that seems counterintuitive since an act and subject would both appear to be something that is obdurately present. Nietzsche's correlation of lightning and the strong man, then, is not wholly appropriate: for the man, unlike the lightning, can choose not to exert his strength.

Part of what informs the positive appearance of the phenomenon of an act is the possibility of its nonexistence.[19] This too is related to the ability of language to assert a negative. "The negative is a peculiarly linguistic marvel," says Kenneth Burke in *The Rhetoric of Religion.* "There are no negatives in nature, every natural condition being positively what it is. . . . you can get the point by stopping to realize that you can go on forever saying what a thing is *not.*"[20] And of course, one of the early complaints against *Waiting for Godot* was that nothing happened. But in the context of an infinite negativity, then, the naming of the act is analogous to the birth of an act. Out of the sense that nothing happens and that there is nothing to be done, action can begin *as though* from nothing. Yet the play does not begin from nothing: after the line "nothing to be done," Vladimir launches out in medias res: "I'm beginning to come round to that conclusion. . . . So, there you are again." He brings out a beginning with evidence of repetition.[21] That division between the negative act and the positive could be described not only by the ways in which language itself is constituted by difference, but also by the way that the material, biological being is not identical to the subject that comes into being through language and signification.[22]

Estragon's statement has a further analogue in the grammar of birth in the sense that the indicative assertion "I am" is contingent upon the passive "I am born." The simultaneity of the two does not diminish the difference nor alter the site of a self *as* the difference. As feminist theorists have been saying for some time, the appearance of the biological person is not what confers an identity. Rather, the discursive poles of active and passive are the limits between which a self appears as a process that negotiates the differences. It negotiates by language and storytelling and by continually alternating between its status as a biological object and as a site of discursive differences.[23]

A grammatic perspective on action suggests that an act is encultured and that one learns how to act as one learns to speak. One becomes a subject through speech, so the self, as George Herbert Mead asserted, is always a social self. The dominance of a teleological view of both action and speech would make it seem that action by definition must have a goal, that the goal is autonomous from a social and linguistic context, and that the failure of action is a failure to achieve that goal. An alternative view is that action is always already occurring and that an agent is more closely related to agency, or the style and quality through which action occurs. The syntactic variation by which agents are related to acts can thus serve to recreate the world by revealing alternative perspectives on what is already present and what has been concealed by conventional grammatical forms.[24]

Hannah Arendt distinguishes, for example, action from labor and work. Speech, she says, not only gives action a name but discloses the human character of the action by answering "who" did this.

> Action and speech are so closely related because the primordial and specifically human act must at the same time contain the answer to the question asked of every newcomer: "who are you?" This disclosure of who somebody is, is implicit in both his words and deeds. . . . Without the accompaniment of speech . . . action would not only lose its revelatory character, but, and by the same token, it would lose its subject.[25]

In other words, action is not only a product, it is productive of subjects. This is another way in which to describe the passive element in the active assertion. As in the statement "I am born," the subject is the product of linguistic acts of representation: the product of a naming. Arendt takes the same dual perspective on active and passive: speech both objectifies the doer (which could be the speaker) and discloses the subject. Yet Arendt seems to presume that there is a perfect conformity between speech and the disclosure of the subject. The conformity, however, is only provisional, since the name of the subject can only correspond to the act of naming. It does not account for the exclusions that are equally possible names. Between taking off his boot and having that happen to him, "Estragon" appears as a discursive version of Estragon. "Estragon" articulates his action as taking off his boot and has concealed other possible "Estragons" by that choice. Arendt does take this into account when she indicates that the actor/sufferer is less an author of itself than a product of the discourse itself:

> the stories, the results of action and speech, reveal an agent, but this agent is not an author or producer. Somebody began it and is its subject in the twofold sense of the word, namely its actor and sufferer, but nobody is its author.[26]

Language is the inert matter that is left over, like the corpse of a living being. At the same time, however, language—through its naming power—is the very thing that brings the act into a form of comprehensible existence. "Being that can be understood is language," says Hans-Georg Gadamer. With the same kind of circularity, that statement can apply here: activity that can be understood is action; but the understanding is linguistically bound. Yet that boundary is also its possibility for change in the same way that the birth of every newcomer offers possibilities for new configurations of action and identity. For the circularity requires the constant transgression of what is already done and understood by what is yet to be done and understood. The fact that action occurs through time is what, in part, makes such transgressions both possible and inevitable. Action transgresses the givens of the world because it does delay, does have multiple temporalities, allows time for questions, doubts, digressions and allows for its own negation.[27] The discursive element of action that makes for an identity, however partial or limited that identity may be, is the same element that allows an act to be renamed, reidentified and have its meanings renegotiated even when it cannot be redone.

In *Waiting for Godot,* the subject that appears in the gap between the concept and the experience—the discursive self—is poignantly articulated by Vladimir's famous speech. That is to say, the sense of negative subject that is not simply replicating the intentionalist subject is one that asks questions. Doubt is the transgression of both the given and the created.

Was I sleeping, while the others suffered? Am I sleeping now? Tomorrow, when I wake, or think I do, what shall I say of today? That with Estragon my friend, at this place, until the fall of night, I waited for Godot? That Pozzo passed, with his carrier, and that he spoke to us? Probably. But in all that what truth will there be? (*Estragon, having struggled with his boots in vain, is dozing off again. Vladimir looks at him.*) He'll know nothing. He'll tell me about the blows he received and I'll give him a carrot. (*Pause.*) Astride of a grave and a difficult birth. Down in the hole, lingeringly, the grave-digger puts on the forceps. We have time to grow old. The air is full of our cries. (*He listens.*) But habit is a great deadener. (*He looks again at Estragon.*) At me too someone is looking, of me too someone is saying, He's sleeping, he knows nothing, let him sleep on. (*Pause.*) I can't go on! (*Pause.*) What have I said?[28]

The active/passive difference describes the combination of responsibility and innocence that inhabits action. That negative subject, operating between, is that which asks questions, is uncertain, queries even its own speech ("What have I said?"), and is the one that refuses final determination by either the given or the created. Rather, the negative subject negotiates with questions, as Vladimir does, in between. In the biological birth, the individual is innocent; but in the second birth through language and social gesture, it is both innocent and responsible: innocent of the language and world of social meanings that predate it and to some extent produce it. But in responding *to* that world, it is also responsible. In taking off his boot, Estragon is responding to a condition: perhaps the boot has a stone in it; perhaps it is too small and pinches his feet. In saying that he is taking off his boot Estragon is making that-which-has-taken-off-his boot. This admittedly small act is a version of how an action is framed both by an awareness of an end (being-toward-death) and the possibility of nonaction and is thus always a transgression of nonbeing and sameness. It suggests that change itself, the openness of an act to the future, is tautological. In his essay, "Cezanne's Doubt," Merleau-Ponty put it this way:

This work to be done called for this life. If I am a certain project from birth, the given and the created are indistinguishable in me and it is impossible to name a single gesture which is merely hereditary or innate. . . . There is no difference between saying that our life is completely constructed and that it is completely given.[29]

For the phenomenologist as for Vico, the given and the created, the active and the passive, are so interconnected as to be indistinguishable. Is this different from some doctrine of predestination? It may be simply a version of Nietzsche's demand to "love one's Fate" and the phenomenologist's view of the relentless coexistence of the given and the created. The idea of an end, in brief, is a function as much as a fact. It teaches that one already is who one will have been.[30] It frames the passive within the active. It says that, however marginal, action and initiative are possible, that by day's end one might have succeeded in taking off a boot; but also that the future is "in the instant" as the future calls forth a self.[31] In the Estragon formulation, what happens is not something imposed by an omniscient author but something created at the moment one does something. In brief, the sense that an action is an attribute of a subject is radically altered by the simultaneity of active/passive voices. The structure of causality shifts from a single source to a complex system.[32]

As Heidegger proposed: "The origin of the work of art is art . . . . because art is by nature an origin."[33] This tautology is not merely perverse; it is an effort to describe a simultaneous operation that is linguistically divided. And in both drama and narrative, the operation employs action for both its discursive limitations and phenomenal openness in which the given and the created are simultaneous. Plot, from this point of view, is a disclosure and an occasion but not a cause for behavior. More specifically, it is an occasion for the resistance to the simultaneity of active and passive, resistance to the completed act, resistance to death. In the act of doubt or delay or resistance, what appears is a self and a character that is a product of that resistance.

What I have hoped to illustrate in this chapter, as I mentioned earlier, is how grammatical formulation—here the active/passive construction—works both to constitute action and to reveal some of its complexity, particularly in the relation of the subject and the act. As the dimension that is most emphatically a creation of language operations (naming and structuring), the act appears to be substantive: to be the name for a real thing. But that reality rests upon a belief in the truth of language, or in the ability of language at least to designate a truth. The disconformities in how the sense of the substantive is created from a language structure indicate how the act itself is an active/passive construction, sustaining its own internal contradictions in which the given and the created are indeed simultaneous and at odds with each other.

Chapter 3

To Do: "I'll Do, I'll Do, and I'll Do"

Macbeth is a play that obsesses on the word *do.*[1] That obsession offers a way to isolate *to do* from the discursive and performative elements of action and to imagine what it would be like if there were such a thing as pure doing. This dimension is perhaps intuitively obvious, even common, to the extent that a current major advertising campaign for athletic shoes can say "Just Do It," presuming on a public awareness of the difference between thinking and doing and the apparent innocence of doing. But if that just-do-it notion has certain affinities with postmodern activities that scorn deliberation, delay, and the ideological constructs of historical action, it has, for Shakespeare's Jacobean England, at least, affinities with demonology and apocalypse.

Even if we had only Macbeth's famous line, "If it were done, when 'tis done, then 'twere well / It were done quickly," (1.7.1–2),[2] the grammatic cycle from subjunctive ("were done") to past indicative ("is done") and back would say something important about doing. That line provides a way to conceive of doing as the entry of an imaginative, or possible, act—the subjunctive—into a material fact, without losing the force of either the fiat or the hypothesis. This is the realm in which the imagined act collapses into a material, real one, with uncanny results. I am going to suggest that the features of Macbeth's articulated and enacted desires for sovereignty, as well as the demonic qualities within the world of the play, can help identify the characteristics of doing as a dimension of action that coalesces future, past, and present and identifies doing with being. The uncanniness of that identification arrives through the plotted mechanism of the relation between Macbeth and the witches, whose visibility for each other reveals the territory of consciousness where material and imaginative action is indeed one thing.

The line quoted above comes from the First Witch, just before the three meet Macbeth. In describing what she'll do to that sailor whose wife wouldn't share her chestnuts, the First Witch promises:

> But in a sieve I'll thither sail,
> And like a rat without a tail;
> I'll do, I'll do and I'll do.

(1.3.8–10)

A frightening threat? First Witch does not yet say *what* she'll do. In isolation, this last line identifies a sense of doing as that which has no object. Such lack signals the emptiness of the verb itself. While active, it has no particularities, only force.

The line has caused commentators some difficulty in accounting for just what it is that the witches will do. The question for Kittredge, for example, is whether the witch will transform herself to get aboard the pilot's ship and cast a spell on him, whether as a rat she'll gnaw through the hull and cause the boat to leak like a sieve (Clarendon), or eat the rudder and cause it to drift (Grierson). Kittredge is fairly sure she means just to lay a spell on the captain, not to scuttle the ship.[3]

Such concerns seem slightly curious. The various possibilities offered by the commentators would seem to assume the witches really will do some thing—or will do something real—to that captain because of his ungenerous wife. But what, to me, seems especially witchlike about this threat is the lack of a direct object for the verb. Those early commentators add on the hypothetical particularity instead of looking precisely at the force of the *lack* of an object of doing. Colloquially, there is either enormous threat or enormous impotence in the failure to name the act by designating just what will be done. With King Lear, the impotence of his rage shows when he claims, "I will do such things—What they are yet I know not, but they shall be / The terrors of the earth! (*King Lear* 3.1.280–82). In *Macbeth* the threat of the witches is also open, but they seem more potent, perhaps because the horror of their power is in doing itself.

An object grammatically extends the verb into an act that takes time, in the sense that it takes time to travel from the verb to the accusative, creating a certain space. Such temporal extension in grammar—"I'll do *that*"—makes the act open to conditions of two parts, verb and object, and hence open to modification, question, and intervention: in short, open to change, dialogue, and response in a human, political realm. The verb without an object, on the other hand, like a monad, is both obdurately closed to negotiation and indefinitely open.[4]

If one knew that the witch were planning to gnaw the hull on that ship, for example, one might make plans to prevent her, or at least to fix the hole. But with no identification of what she'll do, there is no way to counter the act. And most particularly in the context of a nonhuman (i.e., nondialogic being), there is no way to speak back to her threat. The curse is not dialogic and language is pure power. In the absence of extension, language itself becomes something like an automaton, whose very horror consists in its refusal to negotiate. It can only do itself. Incantation in particular is a deed of language. Indeed, such autonomic assertiveness is the basis of most horror films in which monsters like the Blob, the Alien, or the Zombie, are terrifying because they just "do what they do": absorbing, consuming, hacking, or slashing the world in their paths, they are unstoppable by conventional means, and often enough their acts are eponymous. To name the monster is to name the mode of its destructive activity. Thus, the Blob blobs, or Jaws jaws,[5] toward the total destruction of the world. Macbeth, in fact, is portrayed as just such a monster before he ever appears, "with his brandish'd steel, / Like Valour's minion, carv'd out his passage ... Till he unseam'd him from the nave to th' chops" (1.2.17–22). Before the end of the play, Macbeth will identify a unique mode of killing.

In making Macbeth a character who wants to just do it, Shakespeare shows him approaching an apocalyptic vision of action that sees a "deed without a name," or at least a deed without a name other than "Macbeth." The plot of *Macbeth* traces his desire for the point at which the thought makes the deed a fact, a done. As he puts it in act 4,

> Time, thou anticipat'st my dread exploits;
> The flighty purpose never is o'ertook
> Unless the deed go with it. From this moment,
> The very firstlings of my heart shall be
> The firstlings of my hand. And even now,
> To crown my thoughts with acts, be it thought and done.
>
> (4.1.144–49)

The Macbeth who early on would seem to be conscientious, morally opposed to regicide, and thoughtful, in fact disappears entirely after the murder of Duncan and reappears, as he was first described, as a killing machine. Becoming sovereign, in Macbeth's case, means both that he takes Duncan's place and that by the murderous deed he removes the distinguishing features of an individual and begins, more and more, to "look like the time," as though time itself were an invasive force that possessed him and took over his body. Macbeth's desire, in brief, becomes articulated as an image of time in that invocation, "be it thought and done." He has, before the end of the play, fulfilled Lady Macbeth's demand upon him: "To beguile the time, look like the time." When she speaks the line, she of course means to keep appearances appropriate to the occasion ("Bear welcome in your eye, your hand, your tongue"). To "look like the time" is a strange phrase, because of course time has no appearance. But that is just what Macbeth gives it. He traps time in those visible signs of his body, to make it one with exteriority.

In *Macbeth*, the word for the collapse of temporal distinctions is *success*,[6] with all its attendant equivocal meanings at play between the sense of achievement and completion and the sense of consequence, between finality and futurity. In Kierkegaardian terms, it suggests that Macbeth is making the *overleap* of faith, in the sense that he is trying to encompass his fatality from a standpoint of futurity. He invokes time as though attempting to remove himself—the linguistic subject that is the product of language, law, and conscience—from the deed. He would "unknow" himself as a split subject, or, in Empson's words, "to do the deed without knowing it."[7]

Macbeth as a doer functions only in totalities—all active on the battlefield, all passive in the kingdom of choice. In the speech, "If it were done when 'tis done," he deliberates not about the means to an end, which is what Aristotle claims is the basis of deliberation, but about the end itself. The desire for the end, in other words, is an apocalyptic wish for the end of time as extension and the presence of time as totality. The difference between Hamlet and Macbeth is that Hamlet is caught up in deliberation of what means to use to achieve the right action. But Macbeth is entirely caught in ends: he is entranced with finalities and teleologies, not with means. He wonders less about whether the end is right than whether it is possible. The telos of Macbeth's action is a state of being that overrides sequence, and such a state can only be imagined; it cannot be thought through. It can take no time because it is time.

Because Macbeth is such an extremist, he is a more difficult character to play on stage than most audiences recognize. For he does not simply alternate between active and passive, or between warrior and poet; he resides as a character at the extremities of these positions all the time. He presents the simultaneity of the active and passive as absolutes and this makes him oddly a character without qualities. He is a character who *does* look like the time, which has no features. Qualities arise out of a response to the contingent world, and Macbeth scarcely functions in a contingent context. Even the moments that betray a conscience speak out of an apocalyptic conscience more than an ethical one, though in performance an actor can certainly portray ethical qualms. There is of course the famous scene with Lady Macbeth in which he seems to resist the very idea of murder. When he considers that "as his host" he should "against the murtherer shut the door, not bear the knife myself," he is clearly against the murder. But that very clarity is what reinforces the field of the absolutes in which Macbeth consistently functions. He speaks of either/or, not of doubt, not of questions. His language does not rest in deliberation of the point but proceeds immediately to the vision of trumpet-tongued angels and Pity striding the blast.

The Macbeths I have seen on stage tend to invest him with some particularity that the role only partially supports. This of course is inevitable, since actors bring qualities and particularities of their own visibility to a role. Usually the actor alternates between extremes, between the warrior and the poet, the ambitious overreacher or the uxorious sod, with greater success in one or the other. But the text combines the extremes, and therefore resists both particularity and peripety. The textual Macbeth does not appear to change at any point (where Hamlet, alternatively, *is* all change), as much as he simply increases his identity as a killer, as States has suggested,[8] like those devouring horror monsters.

One consequence of relinquishing one's will and doubt and deliberation to time, chance, and futurity, and of releasing oneself wholly to the operation of time and fatality, even in a dramatic character, is to lose the aggregate particularities that make for complexity, variation, and differences. The absence of evidence of deliberation and the conformity of his will with chance and the supernatural leave

Macbeth almost faceless, free of what Beckett called "the comic relief of features" that interrupts and disfigures "the luminous projection of subject desire."[9] To be sure, his face is "as a book wherein men may read strange matters," but that face is an expression not of character as much as of those demonic forces that carry him along. The farther he gets from a social context, the more out of place his particularities seem. Perhaps the text's own obsession with clothes and manhood are a way of pointing at the disappearance of particularity. The more closely Macbeth resembles the time, the more he needs coverings in order to appear, like the Invisible Man. And perhaps this is why, apart from theatrical convention, he disappears from the stage for the period in which his deeds are most heinous.

Now the First Witch does eventually say what she will to do to the sailor she curses in the first act.

> I'll drain him dry as hay;
> Sleep shall neither night nor day
> Hang upon his penthouse lid;
> He shall live a man forbid.

(1.3.18–21)

This clearly has nothing to do with turning into a rat and gnawing a hole in the hull, except metaphorically. Metaphor is certainly the point, as that sailor and his wife quickly transfer to Macbeth and his. A realist might say that this witch knows only one thing to do: drain men of life, make them sleepless, to "dwindle, peak, and pine," thanes and sailors alike. Indeed, the singularity of the witch's curse translates to the singularity of the consciousness with which Macbeth becomes one with the work of his hands, and the notion of a split subject, which is to say a linguistic one, dissolves into images of blood:

> this my hand will rather
> The multitudinous seas incarnadine,
> Making the green one red.

(2.2.60–61)

Macbeth after the murder becomes endlessly wakeful to the endless visible world, seeing all as "one red." The witch has fulfilled the curse upon the sailor, turning Macbeth toward the automatism that characterizes her language, as though, zombielike, he embodied the incantation, "I'll do." The doing of the deed—the doing itself, without an object—eliminates the discursive form of language and replaces that form with images.

Isolating the visible from a discursive context, that is, renders visibility as a site of endless surface in which nothing is hidden. There is no depth perception, no special perspective, no foreground, middle ground, or background, no respite, and no space of difference in which a speaking subject might emerge. There is no relief from seeing, no blinking, no sleep, no alternative when discourse gives way to image. Through this isolation, the visible image no longer represents something else or something elsewhere. It has no second nature in language but is radically itself. Doing is measured, furthermore, not in terms of signification but in terms of statistics and facts. It is literally obscene: for the open eyes, the plane of the visible has no boundaries. When there is no recourse to the invisible, there is no appeal to the network of social meanings and contexts that make the visible signify. This is the stuff of nightmares.

If it is impossible, in the waking world, to eliminate completely, except in madness, the delays of thought, speech, and the intrusion of the invisible, which create a space apart from the wholly visible, it is nevertheless possible to imagine the horror of the endlessness of objects, the collapse of discursive delay and the obdurate surfaces of visibility. In the field of vision and visibility a subjective perspective (the view from the inside) cannot be distinguished from the objective perspective (the view from a distance). The result is that there is no view at all, only, as the French might say, *spectacle*. To know the deed in its purely spectacular appearance, however, is to avoid or not to know the self in its discursive, rhetorical, and social negotiations. Visual knowledge eclipses the self-knowledge and the self that is born in language. So Macbeth laments after the murder of Duncan: "To know the deed, 'twere best not know myself."

If the witches were not real—that is to say, visible—it would be easy to reduce Macbeth's character to simple, ethical evil. But there may be something about their very visibility that gives a clue to why Macbeth does what he does. The presence of the witches for Macbeth provides the images for the depth and force of desire that makes ethical terms like *ambition*, as States notes, "overdetermined."[10] For ambition is something like an ethical veil, concealing the adamantine nature of desire situated in the visible, *as* the visible, on the order of fetish. Macbeth learns his ambition by seeing them and, even more importantly, being seen by them. In a kind of "mirror exercise"[11] he follows the motions of the image such that he cannot tell if chance, vaulting ambition, the witches, Lady Macbeth, or he himself is starting the motion. In some sense, the witches serve to introduce what René Girard has named "mimetic desire."[12] But the mimetic duplication occurs in and because of sight. The demonic nature of the mutual regard is echoed in a phrase attributed to Nietzsche at the beginning of the film, *The Abyss*, which says, "When you look long into the abyss, the abyss also looks at you."

The idea of a view implies the privileged spot of subjective interiority and the separation of the viewer from the viewed. Looking out at the world from the isolation of the specialness of the individual, the world is out there at a distance from the secret recesses of interiority. But spectacle implies a kind of participatory extravaganza in which the seer and the seen are joined in the same stuff that is the matrix of visibility:

> since vision is a palpation with the look, it must also be inscribed in the order of being that it discloses to us; he who looks must not himself be foreign to the world that he looks at. . . . It suffices for us for the moment to note that he who sees cannot possess the visible unless he is possessed by it, unless he *is of it* [*Uerprasentierbarkeit*, of the flesh], unless by principle, according to what is required by the articulation of the look with the things, he is one of the visibles, capable, by a singular reversal, of seeing them—he who is one of them.[13]

Visibility is a condition in which one both possesses and is possessed. It requires a mutual regard. It is through their visibility, not some secret occult power, that the witches possess Macbeth. But what is to be made of the fact that at the initial encounter, Banquo too sees the witches? One important difference, at least in keeping with the theoretical point, is that in the first meeting, the witches hail Macbeth exclusively. They give him the titles of who he has been and will be, while they do not hail Banquo at all, as though he sees them but they do not see him, so he is not possessed by them. In this sense, the function of being hailed, or named, overlaps the function of being seen and reinforces the idea that it is mutual sight (or gaze) that initiates demonic possession.

Visibility, like being hailed, therefore, is not a choice. Such a fact may account for how consciousness is structured to include more than itself without escaping itself, to have elements of self-deception or otherness within. The visibility of the other draws Macbeth "into the sere, the yellow leaf," fulfilling the curse to have him "dwindle, peak, and pine." Just as the mythical Gorgon, Medusa, destroys her attackers when they look directly at her, the mutual regard of Macbeth and the witches suggests the enormous danger of the unmediated glance. It creates a state of trance, in which a speaking consciousness is struck dumb by visions. The trance is the mode of the visionary for whom there is no difference between the subject and its activity, between thought and deed. It is the mode of the one who can move from the thought of murder to visions of apocalypse where

> Pity, like a naked new-born babe,
> Striding the blast, or heaven's Cherubins, hors'd
> Upon the sightless couriers of the air,
> Shall blow the horrid deed in every eye,
> That tears shall drown the wind.
>
> (1.7. 21–25)

Macbeth is as overwhelmed by the image of conscience as he is by the sight of the Weird Sisters. He is caught, so to speak, by the objects of his own sight, whatever those objects might be, and is unable to ask any questions. Macbeth is consistently working in the world of images, not of questions. His ambitions, his conscience, as well as his fears are formulated by phenomenal appearances, so he is entirely credulous when the Weird Sisters show him conjured images of kings. He accepts the ocular as proof, no matter how unreal that ocular proof would appear to reason or how much it may deserve to be questioned. The notion of a deed and of a doing correlates, in other words, with the notion of images as atemporal objects, insofar as they "take" no time. The visible image encompasses a totality that resists questions even more than narrative closure.

By their presence, the witches embody the very element of motivation that is other than or lost to thought, unapproachable and unassimilable. In a very concrete sense, the irreducibility of those bodies on stage replicate the irreducibility of desire: desire that is infinitely transformable and shape-shifting, but always, at least in certain terms, a product of the Other, the unnameable. Yet it is desire in action, not desire in reserve. The witches, like the deed, are without a name and an identity; they can be seen but not considered or thought about. Psychological criticism gave the twentieth century a vocabulary for accounting for them as manifestations of Macbeth's own ambition, as external projections of an internal desire. Even the moralistic point of view from A. C. Bradley, who went a long way in defining character as the central issue, saw that Macbeth's character derived in large part from his surround, from a dramatic world in which the witches and Lady Macbeth are possible. Dowden, more formalistic, asserted that the reiteration of "foul and fair" by Macbeth in 1.3, repeating the witches' "Fair is foul and foul is fair," establishes the connection "between his soul and them."[14] Historians prefer to look at the beliefs in and about witches in the sixteenth and seventeenth centuries and to look at the actuality of their status in the social, legal, and imaginative world.

The problem for so many is that having recognized how thoroughly intertwined Macbeth and the witches are, it seems imperative to account for the ontological status of those entities. William Empson, after rehearsing the concerns of Dover Wilson and Bradley about just *when* Macbeth's murderous thoughts occur, rightly suggests that the very ambiguity of the moment is just the point.[15] Witches, that is, are a category for the ambiguous, unidentifiable, uncanny motives that seem to be apart from the person predicate. After they disappear, Banquo wonders,

> Were such things here, as we do speak about,
> Or have we eaten on the insane root
> That takes the reason prisoner?

>   (1.3.83–85)

Banquo clearly considers what generations of future critics have pondered: the equivocal status of the witches as potentialities embodying either independent "demonic" forces or projections of an hallucinatory fungus; signs of madness or manifestations of a potential for evil already residing within Macbeth. Banquo most certainly shares the vision and, unless the moment is a *folie à deux* or it demonstrates Banquo's special insight into Macbeth's real nature, it would be difficult to reason away the public forum for the appearance of the hags. Yet it is important to remember that they only possess the one for whom the gaze is mutual.

The psychological justifications, unlike Banquo's question, explain away the reality status of the witches by demonstrating their purely symbolic function. It is not that they do not have a symbolic function, but their reality function is more interesting, for it is their manifestation itself that speaks of the otherness of desire. In other words, if the witches are only symbolic projections or manifestations of some inherent potentiality within Macbeth's character, then their power is at most referential, deferring to some notion of the real Macbeth residing behind his actions. This perception reduces them to a delusional feature of Macbeth qua person and devalues their power, as though he could overcome their influence with clear moral will. Their reality function, conversely, is to be a force of both a real and an imaginary in the "palpation with the look." In concert with that function, they demonstrate the quality, the demonic aspect, of the deed: and deed *is* inhuman because it is without the doubt, delay, or hesitations of discourse. It has no outside or privileged view.

Of course, the witches do have a textual history from Holinshed, who reports the story of their prophecy to Macbeth and Banquo. Shakespeare appears to have lifted the witches' appearance as well as the words from the *Chronicles of Scotland*, as "three women in strange and wild apparell, resembling creatures of elder world," hail "Makbeth thane of Glammis . . . thane of Cawdor . . . and heereafter shalt be king of Scotland." And even Holinshed fails to make sense of the encounter:

> This was reputed at the first but some vaine fantsticall illusion by Mackbeth and Banquho . . . but afterwards the common opinion was, that these women were either the weird sisters, that is (as ye would say) the goddesses of destinie, or else some nymphs or feiries, indued with knowledge of prophesie by the necromanticall science, bicause euerie thing came to passe as they had spoken.[16]

The witches, that is, are historical. Their appearance and predictions are documented, at least. What remains in question is the relation of their appearance to a cause. Strange, symbolic synchronicities do occur, even in the mundane world, and some prophetic statements do come true. That there is no pattern or predictability as to which will and which won't occur is not relevant in this case. Given the uncertainties of causality, is it impossible to say with complete assurance that the murder of King Duffe, as reported by Holinshed, did *not* cause the six sunless months when the

> skie couered with continuall clouds, and sometimes such outragious windes arose, with lightenings and tempests . . . and monstrous sights also [when] horsses in Louthian, being of singular beautie and swiftnesse, did eate their owne flesh, and would in no wise taste anie other meate. . . . a gentlewoman brought foorth a child without eies, nose, hand or foot . . . a sparhawke also [was] strangled by an owle.[17]

Human will is built to overcome this chaos, surely; and rational models of causality demystify the mysterious. Reason and choice do operate, after all. But in the moral world as much as the physical ones, even reason and choice are caught up in fields of coincidence. The nature of action in *Macbeth* seems specifically to attempt to allow for the effect of chaotic causality that makes chance seem causal.

Obviously the witches are a category for otherness that cannot be identified as either exclusively interior or exterior. But the category of otherness includes just those events of chance, or as Lacan names it, the *"tuché"* or "automaton."[18] As an "abject" of a psychic economy—an unconscious object that is expelled from consciousness by the horror of its very otherness—the status of the witch is literally unspeakable. Without resorting to psychoanalytic vocabulary, Terry Eagleton put it this way:

> The witches signify a realm of non-meaning and poetic play which hovers at the work's margins, one which has its own kind of truth; and their words to Macbeth catalyse this region of otherness and desire within himself, so that by the end of the play it has flooded up from within him to shatter and engulf his previously assured identity.[19]

Used in a dramatic economy, witches are a rather effective means of rendering visible something unspeakable, and the problem for their staging is that they cannot be terrifying enough. Some monsters are more terrifying when they are absent. The witches, though, tend to be naturalized by the body of the actors. Still, supernatural beings are excellent dramatic devices. They have instant appeal, quite apart from their ontological status, and that appeal may be due precisely to their antimoral power and their spectacular pleasure in horror.

The alignment of Macbeth and the witches, therefore, says something quite specific and unambiguous about the nature, not just of evil or horror specifically, but of motives in general: that within the world of motives there is an element of the uncanny, unidentifiable, and unspeakable; that motives may occur from the Other that is within. This is what makes Lacan's difficult presentation of the Other so useful, upon occasion, and in its own way, so incomprehensible. Lacan himself refused to name the component parts and identity of that Other and yet situated it in the materiality of the signifying system of language. The Other, like witches, is not there but also not *not* there, in visible, graphic signifiers for the endless, absolute, irreducible nature of desire. The Other is not a thing but a force and function, identified only by its effects.

The apocalyptic nature of doing, that is, cannot be visibly staged for the same reason it cannot be named: it is unrepresentable. Yet, the doing is also not *not* visible. Doing is in excess of the name of action, but it *is* present. "What is't you do?" Macbeth asks the witches. "A deed without a name," they reply. The unnamed deed can only be perceived in an altered state of consciousness. Such a state is most evident in act 4, when they conjure visions of the future for him, calling up images from the cauldron. At this point their prophecies convince Macbeth of his invincibility. He does not see the representation of an unrepresentable as an illusion that nonetheless bears messages of a reality.

Like the dream or the Delphic oracle, the truth of the illusion is borne out not by interpretation but by reality. Macbeth, the visions tell him, will not be conquered until Birnam wood comes to Dunsinane, until he faces one who is not born of woman. Clearly, these are conditions that any reasonable interpreter would know to be impossible. Unfortunately, the fact that his conqueror, Macduff, was indeed "from his mother's womb untimely ripp'd," and the branches from Birnam Wood do move to Dunsinane as shields for a conquering army, tends to confirm the play's own persevering attempts to represent the combination of the uncanny and a material reality. That is, the play makes the impossible real and illusory at the same time, resistant only to interpretation.

That particular combination of an impossible real, then, recalls the peculiar emptiness of the word *do* and its sense of force without specificity. Within the play, at least, that force echos in the sexual implications of doing "it," and the sexualized field in which Macbeth finds (or loses) himself. Calderwood notes:

> when Macbeth emerges from the chamber to announce "I have done the deed," Shakespeare can hardly expect his audience not to register the familiar sexual sense of that expression. Especially not when he has strewn his play with such terms as "done," "deed" and "do," and even provided a Witch who ambitiously asserts "I'll do, I'll do, and I'll do."[20]

The openness of the term *do* is connected in the play to the uncanniness of the female presences and the uncertainty of their force in motivating Macbeth to murder Duncan. Lady Macbeth's blatant references to her own sexuality simply reinforce the correlation or, rather, the simultaneity, of motive, deed, sexuality, and Other in the imploded field of doing. Many productions, indeed, have given the part of Lady Macbeth and a witch to the same actress; some have kept the witches present in all the couple's scenes together; some let all three witches perform Lady Macbeth's part. In each case, the uncanny dimension overlaps the social role of wife and woman as manifest evidence that the mere presence of the female, in her obdurate otherness that is other primarily for the male, is sufficient to suspend conscience and consciousness and to impel him to "do the deed."

Like the formal equivocation ("fair is foul and foul is fair") that pervades the play, the notion of doing that it develops is sexually equivocal. That is to say, the sexuality of Lady Macbeth, the witches, and even Macbeth himself, particularly in light of the concerns for manhood in the language, *charges* the play without quite being thematic. Sexuality itself is equivocal. Just as drink equivocates with lechery, motives and witches also "set on and take off"; persuade and dishearten. Sexual equivocation both is and is not an issue in the play. The appeal of Lady Macbeth and the witches, then, is in part derived from the pleasure of seeing what cannot (or ought not) normally be seen or spoken of. They give, in T. S. Eliot's terms, the "objective correlative" for something that is objectively unavailable, which is the otherness of one's own desire, the desire of the Other, which is desire in action.

Macbeth multiplies motives, as though they approached Macbeth from many directions, including the future. It is a question not of how Macbeth intentionally moves, but of what moves him. To be moved by those motives, Macbeth must suspend conscience and ethical consideration and simply answer the bell that says the deed is *now*. Macbeth is invited, that is, by the clock, but the clock and action do not coincide: the future appears as a past, and together they appear as an absolute deed, a done thing.

> I go and it is done; the bell invites me.
> Hear it not Duncan, for it is a knell
> That summons thee to Heaven, or to Hell.
>
> (2.1.62–64)

What moves him, finally, is the sound of the bell: an apt image for the signal that signifies nothing, or nothing but time, which itself is nothing but the combination of the arbitrary and the inevitable.

That bell that rouses Macbeth to go is the invitation of the now that belongs neither to past nor future. It is sound that announces the time is now. Indeed, that now is the sign for a displacement of consciousness into a neither-nor state, something that Lacan calls "between perception and consciousness."[21] That between state, which Lacan describes in relation to a dream that formed around a knock that eventually woke him, is something in excess of both perception and consciousness. Lacan asks who he is at the moment of the knocking: neither fully the perceiver nor the dreamer, he can, upon waking, only recover the representation or supposition of the knock from the memory of the dream. That who is in suspension, neither conscious in its own present, nor present in its re-representation, but something other than both. It is without a name, working in a temporal anomaly. It is in the order of dream and prophecy. Kierkegaard expresses a philosophical version of the psychological state when he says:

> It would already be a precarious matter, so it seemed to him, for someone to undertake to prophesy. And yet, just as one could have an intimation of a necessity in the past, was it not also conceivable that one could have an intimation of a necessity in the future. Philosophy, however, wanted to do something even more difficult: it wanted to permeate everything with the thought of eternity and necessity, wanted to do this in the present moment, which would mean slaying the present with the thought of eternity and yet preserving its fresh life. It would mean wanting to see what is happening as that which has happened and simultaneously as that which is happening; it would mean wanting to know the future as a present and yet simultaneously as a future.[22]

That kind of consciousness, however, is already a part of Macbeth. Upon his first encounter, he stands, as Banquo puts it, "rapt." This occurs shortly after their first prophecy, in which they announce Macbeth's future as "Thane of Cawdor" and "King hereafter." In being rapt, Macbeth could be said to be caught up in a time warp in which he feels, as Lady Macbeth says, "the future in the instant." It is a time warp that denies extension. Not extending through time, that consciousness is bound to pure presence. But at that point, what does Macbeth *want*? It would seem that he wants precisely not to do, not to take action, but to be taken by it. "If chance will have me king, why chance may crown me / Without my stir" (1.3.144–45).

Another way to say this is that Macbeth wants to be taken along by the autonomy of the Other; taken into the state of doing that is being by the very operations of unrepeatability and unrepresentability that characterize chance. The future, standing for the operations of chance, for the unrepresentable cause, is the uncanny other that is present in doing in which no effort is involved. It is as though, in that trance, his desire is to be recognized by chance, visible to futurity.

To imagine that nothing one does can make a difference; to fear that no act of will can make or create anything apart from destiny; to be excluded from dialogue: this is what it means to believe in witches, to be subject to the nonhuman Other. There is no point to extending one's efforts through willful action if, in fact, there is no extension, if time itself is one thing, if "tomorrow and tomorrow and tomorrow" are creeping in at a petty pace in an infinite repetition of sameness. These are the terms in which there is no temporal motion in action.

At the end of the play, of course, Macbeth comes back to a world of motion and action in his fight with Macduff.

> I will not yield,
> To kiss the ground before young Malcolm's feet,
> And to be baited with the rabble's curse.
> Though thou suppos'd, being of no woman born,
> Yet I will try the last:
>
> (5.8.27–32)

Macbeth is ultimately defeated by the irony built into the atemporal absolute: the irony that even the absolute occurs in the world in which time moves on and in which the logically impossible circumstances—to be conquered by one who is not born by a woman and only when Birnam Wood comes to Dunsinane—turn out to be real.

What returns Macbeth to the world of the actual and of effort is the *irony* that an absolute world, in which an impossibility turns out to be a truth, leaves him with nothing but his own effort to "try the last." But if trying means having to exert effort and to take the time of action, is it not still an echo of what Macbeth has done all along, which is to test the limits of the contingent world against the apocalyptic last?

As Macbeth gives the initial prophecy his attention, he is drawn to the futurity that is of the present moment; drawn to collapse temporal succession in both the kingly and the existential sense, and toward the simultaneity of past, present, and future that encompasses the loss of identity in the hope of sovereignty. The audience perceives a logical succession: the structure of the play allows that Duncan has already named him Thane of Cawdor. But this fact appears to Macbeth as a prophecy, and he is caught up perceiving future and past as reversed.

"A doctrine of attention . . . appears to us to be most perceptive and most respectful of the infinite richness of my motivation," writes

Ricoeur. "Rationality of motives is only a privileged form which the course of motivation adopts in certain favorable cases. . . . It is always attention which creates time, wins time, so that all these voices speak distinctly, that is to say, in a succession."[23] The attentive conditions revealed by *Macbeth* are comprised of hope, recollection, and receptivity. They are not revealed "in a succession," however, but in an order converted by Macbeth's in-between consciousness. The conditions would bear temporal modes in which hope "o'erleaps" the present, recollection becomes "wrought with things forgotten," and receptivity submits to the autonomy of time, but Macbeth aims toward simultaneity. Such confounded attention is perhaps more like fixation that quiets the noise of conscience, doubt, and selfhood. It is a kind of attention that eliminates the time it takes to deliberate.[24] It also accounts for the kind of rapture of the continuing collisions or, rather, collusion, between desire and fatality that confound a linear order of action. And it is an apt description for what is happening at the moment in which Macbeth stands rapt. This notion of attention lends itself precisely to a reality principle in which the objects of consciousness and consciousness are complicit in a mutual regard.[25] That sense in which attention can be a motive accounts for how James Calderwood can say that Macbeth "falls in evil" as others fall in love,[26] for there is a similar withdrawal from volition, replaced by a fixation in which he is simply ready for something to happen to him. His own motives, that is, are happening to him, in the consciousness where fate and desire collide. He opens himself to the occurrence of a willed accident that partakes no less of chance than of hope.[27]

Chance thus appears as a reality principle that involves the incalculable dimension of motives that both do and do not belong to the individual since the individual, like the universe, is fragmented by increasing expansion away from a center. Christa Wolf has said that chance is the "fugitive stuff which no story with a view to seem 'natural' can do without; but how difficult to get it into custody."[28] Patterned chance, however, starts to appear as intentionality. So when Roland Barthes writes about the "Structure of the Fait-divers," he recognizes that the appeal of coincidences, ironies, and patterns in everyday, true-life stories is that they *look* like significance.

Yet just as repetition "limits" the anarchic (or innocent) nature of the aleatory, so luck and mischance are not neutral, they invincibly call up a certain signification—and the moment chance signifies, it is no longer chance; the acme's precise function is this conversion of chance into sign, for the exactitude of a reversal cannot be conceived outside of an intelligence which performs it.[29]

Chance rips the unity of action and identity by tearing apart a character's intentions and the character's ability to fulfill them. But when the dramatic or literary form shows the rupture, it also shows the coordination of character and fate.[30]

If one happened to stumble over an obstruction, that would be not an act, but a mere motion. However, one could convert even this sheer accident into something of an act if, in the course of falling, one suddenly *willed* his fall.[31]

The accident, in other words, might be construed less as pure, arbitrary chance and more as the summation or solution to a set of conditions only some of which are apparent. What appears as chance could well be the manifest function simply of what escapes forms of knowledge, such as the causal relation between murder and global mayhem. By forgetting his contingent, historical, and personal self-identity as Macbeth, Thane of Glamis, and aligning his will with the power of the invisible forces, Macbeth does will the aleatory, yet he cannot simply leave it to chance as a thing separate from himself. He must stir and thereby align his will with chance. This means, however, he eliminates the human element of social action that is characterized by hesitation, delay, consideration, and, hence, representation and repetition.[32]

In *The Aesthetics of Excess*, Allen Weiss discusses the dissolution of identity in the work of Klossowski in the context of Nietzsche's notion of the Eternal Return. In the absence of a God who could guarantee an identity that exists in the remove of an eternal Heaven, he says, the "self becomes the scene of an indefinite series of identities and transformations" where "the self is willed as a fortuitous moment (and no longer a continuous identity)." This task is accomplished through the affirmation of the Eternal Return,

which transforms self identity by inaugurating a sovereign master over time and volition, precisely by willing one's own fortuitous existence. As such, it is the willing of difference, of the
aleatory, which is ultimately incommunicable, since it is lived as
pure intensity without intention. . . . And yet, so that this Recur-
rence not be just one more determination of Being, the Eternal
Return must be forgotten, along with the self which is lost. Thus
the Eternal Return is essentially the possibility of possibility by
being the forgetting of forgetting; otherwise it would be yet one
more sign of the dialectical process instilled as memory.[33]

The extremity of such a condition of sovereignty means that it too is
unrepresentable. Or representable only as intensity, not as intention.
And for *Macbeth* it can only be staged by his complete absence from
the stage in act 4. For that act, he can only be spoken of; he cannot
be shown.

A moment of thought returns for Macbeth occurs in the famous,
brief speech, "Tomorrow and tomorrow and tomorrow." Its very
brevity makes it more poignant, more fragile. But even as he speaks,
the words appear to drain Macbeth of all thought, emptying the
difference supplied by signification, such that his death comes without meaning and without even much feeling. Having brushed the
apocalypse with Macbeth, having at least fictionally eliminated the
gap between thought and action, and between sign and signification,
the play finishes with the claim that "time is free." Once time flows
again, however, Macbeth's doing seems to me almost immediately
nostalgic and glorious in the way that the simultaneous hand and
thought, like the athlete's deed, eliminate duration and leave only a
memory trace in the actual world, a deed without a name.

In the context of dramatic practices, perhaps the clearest articulation of that effect is from Artaud. For in spite of the fact of its textuality, and therefore of its repeatability, *Macbeth* is conjuring a sense
of action as specifically unrepeatable, unspeakable, theatrical.[34] In
attempting to free the theater of texts, Artaud is trying to eliminate
the corpse of action that, like the corpse of Ophelia discussed earlier,
is the object of ethical judgment, text, and form. He is attempting to
describe the unrepeatable and unnameable quality of living action
that is wholly physical, material, and visible. "Beneath the poetry of
the texts, there is the actual poetry, without form and without text."[35]

In his manifesto, he calls for an end to "empiricism, randomness, individualism and anarchy." This apparent paradox, correlating empiricism with randomness and anarchy, is a way of pointing out the cruelty and determinism that constitute the fatality and the mystery of real action. "We are not free. And the sky can still fall on our heads. And the theater has been created to teach us that first of all."[36]

If to name the act is in soine sense to congeal it at a social, moral, or psychological level, the unnameable act is represented by both the witches and Macbeth as having no distinctions or differences that could mark time, duration, or identity and certainly none that could mark good and evil. For all of those marks require repetition and representation. Representation that is empirical is nonetheless anarchic to Artaud because it is a corpse, divested of the determinate forces of life and therefore detached from force and presence and the reality of the senses. The end of representation would, to Artaud, be cruel and chaotic but also generative and creative: living and necessary.[37]

That version of necessity may be found in other contexts that so fascinated Lacan: in the speech of hysterics or in the religious visionaries.[38] These special cases point to a dimension of action that operates purely in the order of signifiers without signification, on the order of the Other as an absolute demand, capable of doing without representation. Artaud wants the visible, nonrepresentational theater to demonstrate that necessity is action as the present, in the present. And that necessity dissolves—or finds irrelevant—distinctions like cause and effect, psychological motives, social judgments, communicative language. If the relationship between Macbeth and the witches is indeterminate, it is because it is not representing some other, true relationship, not an embodiment *of*, but a fact that creates a world. That is, it includes the manifestation of what we now call order and disorder, regularity and chaos, congruity and incongruity, finite and infinite. The science of chaos, like the speculations of phenomenology, suggest that however unrepeatable events in time are— and therefore how free they are from stability and even knowability— events are nonetheless bound.[39]

Macbeth's line, "be it thought and done," identifies action as a fiat. But the order of language can scarcely approach the reality of doing, as the dimension of action bound and determined by the body. When the imaginary dagger appears before Macbeth, he reaches toward it, and it is the gesture itself that makes the deed, however illusory the object.[40] The gesture of his hand binds time to the body in pure presence, forgetting past and future. It is action in body time that makes thought visible not in time but as time. If this has its cruel or demonic side, as Artaud would have it, it is because when thought is exclusively corporeal, there is neither space nor time for judgment.

Macbeth represents a radical form of theatricality in which visibility is the site for identity, motives, and meanings. If it exhibits elements of Artaud's ideal for a nonrepeating, nontextual, bodily, hieroglyphic action, it is nonetheless representational and repeatable. Other plays certainly go further in announcing to an audience the fact that theater is a place for seeing and being seen. But *Macbeth* shows, through the agency of Macbeth, what it is like for the mind to conform to visibility. And that is the rapture of the stage and the image. An audience, too, becomes rapt in the spectacles of the stage, transfixed by the images of what is being done. Events, with their meanings and motives, are translated into the surfaces of visibility, which works alongside and within an act as a structure and performance as an adjustment to the public occasion. When that territory is bracketed and isolated from the extremes of act and perform, it serves as a reminder that one is always "installed in the midst of the visible." "The performance," Herbert Blau says,

> in its signifying succession (not-signified) conceals and erases itself in the motion of its production. And that motion . . . initiates and contains the problematic of the audience, which gathers around this paradox: that the pleasure of seeing . . . is constrained by the desire to see what cannot be seen.[41]

An audience is placed to see not only persons performing as objects but also to see the space in which both performers and the audience are joined and defined, a space that generates both distance and proximity as the same thing:

> It is that the thickness of flesh between the seer and the thing is constitutive for the thing of its visibility as for the seer of his corporeality: it is not an obstacle between them, it is their means of communication. It is for the same reason that I am at the heart

of the visible and that I am far from it: because it has thickness
and is thereby naturally destined to be seen by a body.[42]

The witches of *Macbeth* go far in showing what cannot be seen, just
as Macbeth goes far in showing that the consciousness that inhabits
the visible is consciousness of being, not becoming. In the radical
sense of visibility, the spectacle of theater represents a collapse of
temporal sequence in which action erases itself as it is produced.

The visible dimension answers Wittgenstein's question by saying
there is no difference between the fact that my arm goes up and the
fact that I raise my arm. Intentionality is consumed by fact, by the
done thing. In spite of the distinctions that consider whether we are
really mentioning the same arm, a different arm, an arm governed
by outside forces, or an arm that has changed through time, the
theatricality of the event makes intention identical to fact. This identification is part of what makes theater a dangerous place, since the
only criterion of validity is the ocular proof. Though there may be
no "art to find the mind's construction in the face," the proof is in the
doing that makes that construction appear on the face. On the plane
of the visible will and chance coincide; the responsibility for action
conforms to inevitability; and active and passive voices become images. Spectacle equalizes differences, and in the theater all visions,
like the parade of kings conjured for Macbeth around the cauldron,
are equal. Signifying nothing, those visions cannot be true until the
future is in the instant to show they are real.

Chapter 4

To Perform: "We Must Work!"

One of Chekhov's more ironic lines is Irina Prozorov's exclamation in *The Three Sisters:* "We must work!" Irina claims to have awakened in the morning with everything clear about how one ought to live. But by the end of the play, having worked to exhaustion at the telegraph office, Irina's clarity has gone murky, and her sister Olga keens against the military music of the departing army, "If we only knew. If we only knew." Work certainly represents far more to Irina than working, and the irony arises in the distance between what it represents and what it is in the banality of the world. Such a distance shapes the landscape of virtually all the Chekhovian characters who live, as Bert States has put it, "in the province of the wish, not of the act."[1]

The initial irony of Irina's line in the context of *The Three Sisters* comes out of her innocence as well as her indolence: innocence in presuming that work is a final solution; indolence in arriving at that solution from the comfort of her bed rather than in any actual engagement. That combination can be interpreted as Chekhov's own ironic indictment of the semiaristocratic class he represents in most of his plays. But indolence is not really the problem in *The Three Sisters.* Olga, after all, is working as a schoolteacher, and Irina, by the third act, has taken jobs first in the telegraph office then in the office of the town council. The sisters are not portrayed as lazy in the manner of some of Chekhov's other characters. Ranevskaya in *The Cherry Orchard*, for example, can easily be accused of aristocratic indolence or carelessness as she moves blithely from Paris to Russia, dropping gold coins as she goes.

I want to begin by looking directly at the imperative mood in "We must work!" and discuss how Chekhov identifies the distance between a demand to act and practical action. In that line, it would seem that Irina is attempting to motivate herself, to generate enthusiasm, inspiration, or emotion that would lead to action. Or perhaps she already has the enthusiasm and expresses it in the form of an imperative. Either case betrays a structure of action, as discussed in chapter 2, that places the subject prior to any activity. The same structure, in which a character is determined as an entity apart from its acts and defined as a complex system of emotions and desires, is an important aspect of the historical phenomenon of realism in the theater, as it was implied by Stanislavski and developed to an extreme in American realism of the twentieth century. Although Stanislavski certainly modified his own practices over the course of his career, a dominant sense of realistic character for this century—obviously aided by the insights and theories of Freud—has come from a belief that emotional depth and desire, often inacessible to consciousness, constitute an essence of character. The typical characters of twentieth-century realism are notably unable to act and are hardly emotional virtuosos. They are barely there.[2] Chekhov's characters generally are almost inert. Without discounting the importance of the historical context of Freud, Marx, and revolution, I want only to discuss how Chekhov establishes a sense of interiority in his characters and follows the logic of that interiority to the point of atrophy. My larger purpose is to point toward the difference between a structure of action that is based on a notion of an essential character, and performance.

Desire would seem to be an initiator of action, but Chekhov shows it to be a major obstacle. The structure of desire, moreover, tends to preclude performance and betrays itself as a metaphysical morass in which desire stands in relation to a demand for an absolute. That is, I want to propose that the psychological realism of Chekhov is sustained by an implicit metaphysics and demonstrates the mundane consequences of a metaphysical stance toward action. The metaphysics I mean to illustrate is founded upon a nostalgic desire for wholeness and fusion with an imaginary past, situated by a longing for the sublime. Yet Chekhov also shows alternative modes of action. Some of his other figures are specifically resistent to nostalgia and show both the pragmatic and aesthetic consequences of such resistence. They are figures who play games with self-representation and identity. The further point, however, is that the specific dangers of nostalgia do not necessarily conform to the values that appear through the sisters, nor does the pleasure of play preclude a certain brutality in the characters who can perform. What I want to suggest is that the dimension of performance can be found in both types of characters because performance is not simply a matter of structure, or even of pragmatic action, but of qualities identified by social codes of feeling and perception.

The force of the imperative or demand, articulated by Irina, marks the entanglement of demand and desire. In Lacanian terms, of course, the entanglement is a condition of the relation of an unconscious to the Other. In saying, "We must work!" Irina puts forth an imaginary demand that she and her sisters prove unable to fulfill. Perhaps one thing that Chekhov makes clear in the line is exactly the failure of the imperative exhortation as a motivator, and the impossibility of a simple emotion, intention, or energy to generate an act. Perhaps it simply indicates the impossibility of ever fulfilling the imaginary demand of the Other. Either way, the imperative of "We must work" highlights the subjunctive mood in which the sisters operate: a verbal substitution for actual practice. Chekhov's play makes clear that a mere locution is not a sufficient condition for initiating an act.

In the first act of *The Three Sisters* Irina reports that when she woke up that day, her name day, "everything" was clear to her. She knew how life had to be lived: "A human being has to labour, whoever he happens to be, he has to toil in the sweat of his face; that's the only way he can find the sense and purpose of his life, his happiness, his delight."[3] She then proceeds to an encomium toward the working people that few who work would appreciate, finally celebrating the nobility of the working ox and horse. Irina characterizes work in its ideal form: as a way to fill the time and fill it meaningfully.

The fact that her insight on work appears to have occurred during her morning repose in bed, which Olga says is between seven (when they were taught to rise) and nine (which is her habitual rising time), is Chekhov's own irony toward her insight. Her revelation is derived from the place closest to the wholeness of the womb that the world can provide. Irina speaks from the place of the unified self, the one that is held, protected, and preserved by the safe envelope of the bed. Moreover, it is on her name day: a day that celebrates the baptism into the illusion of a singular identity. In the play, the day is also the anniversary of her father's death, and the ghost of the father presides over the household as a reminder of the time when the family was happy. Olga, the first to speak, says, "It's exactly a year since Father died. A year ago today—May the fifth—it was on your name day, Irina."[4]

Irina's insight, in other words, comes from the position of celebrating her place both in the scheme of things and enjoying the bodily pleasure of lying in and feeling, as well as being conscious of, the wholeness of her self as a given. In such a state, how could she not see the meaning of life? What her insight indicates is the primacy of an image of self over an image of action; it fixates on a sensation of wholeness that is private, interior, and apart from the world and prior to action.

From the morning bed, where the body's comfort reasonably resists getting up and out into the cold, Irina can project work as a whole whose quality is better than and similar to lying in. It becomes the image for a way of being in the world that is both different from lying in bed, because it is imagined out there *in* the world, and the same as lying in bed, because it is projected from there. That the ox and the horse working are better than "the young lady who rises at noon, drinks her coffee in bed, then takes two hours to dress"[5] is perhaps unarguable. But the point for my purposes is not Chekhov's recognition of aristocratic indolence or existential ennui but the way that Irina's image of meaning is tied to an imperative and how that imperative is retied to a prenatal restfulness. Her image as she woke up is how one *ought* to live one's life. The call to action is nostalgically embedded in the enveloping space of bed, a maternal space. She has an imaginary sense of completeness, wholly interior, that coalesces identity and activity into a unity that is identical to the self celebrating the self from bed. And that idea is comfortingly bound to a belief that the meaning of one's life is authorized by the imperative. She *must* work. The authority for this meaning, however, is no more than an image which is no more than a bed-bound project. The body is at once enveloped by the comfort of the bed and imagined to be capable of extending that wholeness into the realm of concrete deeds. The imperative "we must work" has the force of an absolute and is bound to the sense of prenatal, parental paradise that includes both mother and father.

The imperative to work functions as a substitution for the absent will that, if present, would already be engaged in the act. "The will," says Ricoeur, "is a power of decision only because it is a power of motion. . . . we can separate these two functions of the will only by abstraction. . . . A projected willing is an incomplete willing: it is not put to the test and it is not verified. Action is the criterion of its authenticity."[6] In psychoanalytic terms Irina's speech characterizes a longing to make present the absent parents: to recover the wholeness of the maternal other and the law of the paternal that are authentic. The longing, however, does not give her the power of motion. The interiority of desire persists as an imperative that cannot be fulfilled. The ghost of old Hamlet similarly dominates Hamlet's inaction, but the difference between the inaction of Irina and Hamlet is that Hamlet is exteriorizing his revenge all along, playing it out in rhetoric and wit. For Irina, inaction consists of remaining attached to the familial nest.

In her final speech of the play Irina has altered the form of her insight. The idealism of the imperative has become:

> We have to work, that's all, we have to work! Tomorrow I shall go on my way along. I shall take up my teaching post, and devote my life to those who may have some use for it. It's autumn now. Soon winter will come and bring the first falls of snow, and I shall be working, I shall be working.[7]

There is also a difference in the word she uses for the imperative. In the Russian texts, she first uses the word *dolzhen* for "must." In the last act, the word is *nado*. A Russian grammar indicates that *dolzhen* "usually indicates a certain personal obligation or moral obligation from within," while *nado* "often suggests compulsion from the outside."[8] The difference between the verbs traces the difference between a necessity that is self-determined and one that is imposed by the world. The transference suggests that by the end of the play, the internal sense of a demand has become a condition of being-in-the-world, from which there is no escape. That worldliness is both tediously repetitious and endlessly the same.

Hannah Arendt discusses the distinction between work and labor in a related way. Notions of labor specifically can never designate a finished product; labor engages in the maintenance of daily life and daily necessities. Work, contrarily, like handicraft, can be both a process and an object.[9] Labor, then, is what Irina identifies in the final speech: it involves the pain of daily maintenance, not the ideal project. And it involves necessity, not volition or desire. Furthermore, there is no product. It is too daily and laborious. In Elaine Scarry's terms, the boundary conditions of experience are pain and imagining and the word *work* can be part of both pain, as in labor, and pleasure, as in the products of art, imagination, and civilization.

> The more it [work] realizes and transforms itself in its object, the closer it is to the imagination, to art, to culture: the more it is unable to bring forth an object, or bringing it forth, is then cut off from its object, the more it approaches the condition of pain.[10]

Irina's actual work at the telegraph office, which has no object, is thus closer to Scarry's notion of pain and Arendt's of labor. It is the horrifying side of a world empty of an ideal.

The trajectory of the play similarly traces the loss of desire into an ironic emptiness, moving the sisters from the public space of the drawing room, to the compressed space of a shared bedroom, until they are finally displaced to the garden, outside the family house altogether, watching the army depart. The repetition, "we must work, we must work," associated with a decreasing ability to *act*, describes the course of the play from the perspective of entropy, a perspective that links the world of Chekhov with the world of Beckett.

Olga's final words in the play, "If we only knew, if we only knew," similarly betray the desperate desire for the unifying power of knowing: to know would be to know meaning, which would be to know closure and totality, which would mean to know one's own life while living. Her subjunctive wish is to know the effect of a decision before the decision is enacted, to know the meaning of an act before the act is taken, to know the meaning of the life before the life is lived. Within the desire for such totality, the will cannot begin. The desire to know, for Olga, represents the imaginary position of a completed life, and she apparently feels she cannot move until she knows. Her desire is tied to a narrative sense of action that is authorized by an end. With reference to the gravedigger's speech from chapter 1, she would like the coroner's judgment on her life, before it is over.

The total structure, which unites beginning and end, is a condition not simply for Irina on her name day but for the family's own perception of itself and its single desire: "to go to Moscow." In a conversation just prior to Irina's vision of the meaning and imperative of life, she and Olga have concurred on the dream: to go to Moscow. They envision themselves as a unit: one will not move without the others, although Masha may be either an obstacle to their leaving or simply be stuck in the provinces until summer.[11] The point is not that this family is in neea of therapy but that Chekhov is consistently demonstrating the operation of how a fusion in the sense of identity is an obstacle to action.

The action of any individual character in the family is bound to the action, or nonaction, of the others. The ensemble acting work required for actors playing Chekhov is, from this point of view, not an arbitrary ideal of acting as much as a recognition of how the characters in a Chekhov play are more bound to each other than are characters in other plays. Their action, or nonaction, is bonded in spite of an appearance of isolation. The familial and devotional ties among Chekhovian characters condition the ability of any one character in the familial group to act in the sense of taking initiative, because to do so would mean to sever ties and, in psychological terms, to individuate. Generally, only those characters already outside the familial bonds are able to act (Natasha in *The Three Sisters* or Lophakin in *The Cherry Orchard*), and their actions are conceived as brutal though pragmatic. The pragmatists are not held in thrall to the unity of familial inertia or to the need for meaning. They do not conceive the world from the idle position of the morning bed; and they have not come from the privileged world of the family bed. They have no imperative, no call to action. They are already fragments. It is the familial and traditional ties that appear impossible to break up.[12]

The geography of the play suggests further that the Prozorov family lives in marginal Russia, where Moscow is the center.[13] This geography, given the symbolizing habits of realism in the early twentieth century, quickly converts to identify the psychic condition of the family. Symbolic techniques in general, that is, contain a means of correlating the personal, psychic economies with a cultural economy. For Chekhov specifically, the further issue is how a relation between center and margin delineates the structure of thought that prevents motion. *The Three Sisters* enacts a kind of geometry of thought by symbolizing a structure of desire that is at the foundation of an inhibition: a structure that defines and enacts what it is *like* to live where everything is conditioned by the authorizing force of an absent and unattainable and therefore imaginary center; where one's place is defined and determined in relation to that image. The geographic and logistical problem for the sisters is difficult enough: they don't even live near the train that could take them to Moscow. But when that geography is duplicated in the structure of thought, what becomes apparent is that the center is a gravitational pull toward a nonexistent and, perhaps, towards nonexistence.

Moscow is the name by which nostalgia for the past itself throws itself forward as a terminal ideal. It is an interior space. The sisters are frozen within the enclosure of nostalgia and the image of Moscow. So Moscow has the character of an absolute; it is a truth created by the sisters, a *folie à trois*, not a place with roads and buildings and fruits and dogs and people and samovars just like the ones they have in the country. Because Moscow is not a contingency but an ideal and an idea, it has no dimensionality in time and space, which is to say no physical reality, no concreteness, no specificities— and there are no train tracks that lead to an idea. Moscow, in short, is a metaphysical, imaginary, and symbolic center, associated with the girls' dead father. In the play it signals a difference between material and imaginary realities, a difference that situates endless desire.

It is, of course, possible to identify the nature of that desire in psychoanalytic terms. As Lacan puts it, "The symbol manifests itself first of all as the murder of the thing, and this death constitutes in the subject the eternalization of his desire."[14] But one need not refer just to psychoanalysis to define the habit of accommodating loss or absence by unifying it in a symbol. While psychoanalysis would find symbolic substitutions and absences everywhere and may usefully account for how Moscow works as a symbol for the sisters, a philosopher like Richard Rorty suggests that the unity of the symbol is an attempt to take in *possibility*, not just the absent father. In his idea of beauty he indicates that there are alternative strategies for coping with the multiple contingencies of the world of appearances. He helps identify both how the unifying symbol works and the fact that it represents a failure to operate ironically within the contingent, actual world. And it is the manner of working within those contingencies that I will later want to identify in terms of performance.

Beauty, depending as it does on giving shape to a multiplicity, is notoriously transitory, because it is likely to be destroyed when new elements are added to that multiplicity. . . .

By contrast, sublimity is neither transitory, relative, reactive, nor finite. The ironist theorist, unlike the ironist novelist, is continually tempted to try for sublimity, not just beauty. This is why he is continually tempted to relapse into metaphysics, to try for one big hidden reality rather than for a pattern among appearances. . . . The sublime is not a synthesis of a manifold, and so it cannot be attained by redescription of a series of temporal encounters. To try for the sublime is to try to make a pattern out of the entire realm of *possibility*, not just of some little, contingent, actualities.[15]

Certainly Chekhov shows many of his characters caught up in possibility, seeking the sublime. As Vershinin says, putting it in nationalist frame: "a Russian is peculiarly given to an exalted way of thinking, but tell me, why is it that in life he falls so short?" In Rorty's terms, he falls short because manifold life falls short of the unitary idea and unifying force of the description of sublime that patterns the totality of past, present, and future, not just "little, contingent actualities." Yet the patterning of those little actualities is what Chekhov—as opposed to his characters—does show, and what constitutes their actual performance.

Indeed, Chekhov's characters are constantly shown as held in the thrall of the sublime and the enervating power of the *possible* even as they live in the manifold of actuality. In this sense, Chekhov's sisters are practicing metaphysicians who, unlike Hamlet and Macbeth, demonstrate how those metaphysics operate as a daily trap in a daily way, and how devotion to the idea paralyzes action. Metaphysics is not, in this view, a philosophical abstraction: it operates in the realms of the ordinary because it is grounded in the dynamics of desire and demand. The desire that the sisters hold to is entangled with the lost world of the parents that is reconstituted as an ideal. The thrall of Moscow thus is the thrall of language and thought that turns a world exclusively into concept. It contains them to the same degree that they contain it.

Like many Chekhovian characters, Vershinin, the philosophiz-

ing soldier from Moscow, is given to rapturous displays about time
and change. Such characters are often taken to indicate the emptiness
and futility in the present conditions of the Chekhovian world. But
if these characters mark, in part, the moody nostalgia in the
Chekhovian scene, they also locate within the plays an ironic perception on the idealizing habits of other characters.

> When a little more time has passed, say, two or three hundred
> years, then people will look at our present-day life with horror
> and contempt, and all this will seem awkward, difficult, very
> uncertain and strange. . . . a time will come when everything will
> change to your way, people will live like you, but then later, you
> too will be outmoded, people will appear who will be better than
> you.[16]

Vershinin imagines a future that will look upon his present in terms
of what the characters themselves seem to feel about their lives: horror, contempt, awkwardness, uncertainty, and strangeness. He first
idealizes the present of the three sisters, then imagines them too as
outmoded in terms of a future perception. Feeling "the future in the
instant," Vershinin has a convoluted sense of past, present, and future that displaces the actual and replaces it with a philosophizing
mood. But in fact, Vershinin is closer to Rorty's notion of the ironist-
novelist who recognizes the partiality of all idealized notions or totalizing theories, for he is articulating how the reality of the passage of
time disintegrates all ideals. In spite of his philosophizing, furthermore, his place in the army allows him to move. The difference
between Vershinin and the three sisters is that his philosophizing is
just an exercise. It does not hold him.

Among the characters of this play, Vershinin is the pragmatic
idealist, therefore, not a metaphysician. What appears in his character as selfishness or hypocrisy or some refusal to commit to Masha
or to leave his ever-suicidal wife and children, is, in these terms, an
ability to play the contingencies, to enjoy his projections and extrava-
gant hopes for the future but not get caught by them and, more
certainly, not to identify himself with the future. Vershinin recognizes himself and his own desires as contingencies of his historical
moment. While his speeches about hope and possibility articulate an
empty philosophy, they are only speeches; in terms of Vershinin's

capacity to act, which is to say, to move on, they are only words, his "chev'ril gloves" of wit. Vershinin performs his philosophical flights but is not bound by them. Words, for Vershinin, are easy to come by and easily dismissed because they are not attached to metaphysical categories of Moscow or to his body. What governs Vershinin's action is the army: the army, the driving force that is constantly on the move and because it is always on the move allows for the luxury of poetic flight without the dangers of becoming lost in space.

If the initial symptom of the unitary condition was Irina's imperative "We must work!" the further symptom is the all-encompassing mood that dominates the play. That is to say, the mood that is so often tossed off as a way of describing Chekhov's plays, as a way of excusing the fact that nothing happens, could rather be a way of describing what does happen. Mood is thus a style of action and the medium through which characters in Chekhov are perceived. It pervades their own represented consciousness, and that of an audience. Through mood, Irina, Olga, Masha, and the others are acutely aware of their pure existence apart from its contingent, historical circumstances, and of the inescapability of being here. And that constant awareness is tied, consequently, to the further awareness, for Irina, Olga, and Masha, of not being elsewhere. As Bruce Wilshire summarizes the Heideggerian description of mood:

> The categorical condition which Heidegger locates in all attunements and moods is *Befindlichkeit*. Difficult to translate, it can perhaps be said to mean that one always finds oneself, one is always present to oneself, however obscurely or inarticulately. This manifests itself as mood. What we ordinarily think to be our "center" is really a hum of mood in which we are lost in a mimetic periphery which we cannot acknowledge. . . . even in that dull satiation with self which we might call a flat or moodless state, still that is a mode of finding oneself in the world, of being present to oneself; it is the mood of blankness and satiation. The self cannot escape itself. Because it is a being-in-the-world it cannot be and escape the world.[17]

Seen in these terms, the three sisters themselves constitute the center that cannot move outside itself because it is "lost in a mimetic periphery." This mimetic periphery seems to describe accurately the condition of the Prozorov family, which is simultaneously marginal and too much present to itself. Another way of describing the functional aspect of mood, in other words, is to say that if the sisters are dominated by the longing for meaning, beauty, love, poetry, work, or Moscow, longing constitutes their consciousness and their action. Their attunement or care is in the inescapable fact of their being-in-the-world and of not being in Moscow. For the three sisters, to be is to long for because their consciousness is subsumed in nostalgia. More importantly, their awareness of themselves as longing-beings has displaced consciousness from the fragmentary world of activity and into the totalized, mood-dominated self-consciousness. Such a placement of consciousness, initially dominated by the authority of their father, is a displacement into the longing for the return of the familial nest, for the enclosure of meaning, authority, and comfort. The totalizing effect of mood comes from the awareness of a self as being (here or present) in the world, combined with the sense of all that is absent or there, elsewhere, only in possibility.

An alternative form of desire is play, in which totality is contingent upon a delimited time and space where meaning is represented as self-representation, and dissembling and the divisibility of the self is a primary condition for action. "Life," says Ricoeur, "is enjoyed (*erlebt, sentie*) rather than known: a certain diffuse affectivity reveals my life to me before my reason can explain it to me."[18]

Fedotik, though a minor character, is the artist of the play. He takes pictures. That is, he plays with representation; he duplicates reality for the fun of it. He breaks up the unitary thrall of the family scene by isolating it in an object or work that combines the imaginary and the concrete in a mediated form. Fedotik is free of nostalgia, but he has such freedom, perhaps, because he is not part of the family scene: he is only the recorder of it. The photos, in other words, indicate the power of representation itself to play within both materiality and imagination, reality and temporality, by creating a "pattern of appearances," not a sublime unity.[19]

Indeed, Fedotik is consistently seen as playful. He brings a toy top to Irina on her name day in act 1. In act 2, he has bought her toys, crayons, and a penknife. He plays cards ("another game of patience") and tells her fortune: "You see, the eight falls on the two of spades. [*Laughs*]. That means you won't go to Moscow."[20] At the end of the act, finding the wretched child, Bobik, ill and the celebration canceled, he promises to bring the child some toys. In act 3, after the fire, Fedotik dances and laughs during his announcement that everything he had —guitar, photography equipment, letters, even the notebook he planned to give Irina—has been burned. His dance counteracts the loss and refuses nostalgia. By act 4, he seems to have recovered some equipment and the notebook, because he takes a final snapshot of Irina and gives her a little notebook with a pencil. Irina, ever hopeful, says, "Someday we shall run across one another." But Fedotik, the playful realist, says, "In ten or fifteen years, perhaps? By then we shall hardly recognize one another, we'll greet each other coldly . . . [takes snapshot]. Stand still . . . Once more, for the last time." Fedotik, that is, functions in the play in a mode of action entirely different from those around him. At his departure, he is the realist who recognizes the impossibility of maintaining the present moment in the future and is thus free of both the nostalgia for the past and the hope for the future. He is a performer who takes and gives pleasure, such that his style or quality could be called pleasurable.

If Fedotik is a figure of the happy clown, the character Solyony is a figure of the melancholy one. Both of them stand apart from the family scene as *eirons*, but Solyony has adopted what could be called the negative aspect of representation and performance. Chekhov has given him a character that repeats a conventional figure of Russian literature: the melancholic ironist who suffers and thinks too much—the Hamlet figure of Russian literature whose mind and motive is obscure, convoluted, and remote.

Solyony's speeches are few, but when he does speak it is to puncture the postures of the moment. After Tuzenbach's encomium to the future of the working classes ("in twenty-five or thirty years everyone will work") Solyony says, "Twenty-five years from now you'll no longer be here, thank God. In two or three years you'll die of apoplexy, or I'll lose my temper and put a bullet through your head, my angel."[21] Like Fedotik's card playing prescience, Solyony's is prophetic and realistic and serves to break the illusions of the moment. His Hamletic aspect, however, appears when he speaks as though he were suffering "that within which passeth show," as in this exchange: "If a man philosophizes, you'll get philosophy, but if a woman, or a couple of women, start philosophizing—it's like pulling taffy!" Masha asks, "What do you mean by that, you impossibly dreadful man?" and he replies: "Nothing. He no sooner cried 'Alack' than the bear was on his back."[22] He is commenting continually on the condition of the Prozorov world with his passing "peep, peep, peeps" in a kind of verbal killing off of sense, when Tuzenbach attempts his philosophizing. He has the wit to say about the child Bobik, the object of Natasha's excessive devotion, "If that child were mine, I would have fried him in a skillet and eaten him."

The specific motivation for his behavior, of course, becomes clear in act 2 when he professes his love for Irina. Her rejection provides the dramatic linchpin that will finally destroy even her compromised happiness with Tuzenbach ("There must be no happy rivals . . . I swear to you by all that's holy, I will kill any rival").[23] The failed love might constitute the motive for his actions and could be sufficient explanation for his behavior. But within that stated motive, Solyony has adopted Lermontov as his model. His character, in other words, has a literary source, and he is performing the qualities out of Lermontov.

When I'm alone with someone, it's all right, I'm like anybody else, but in company I'm despondent, timid and . . . talk all sorts of nonsense. Nevertheless, I am more honest, and more noble than many, many others. And I can prove that. . . . I have never had anything against you, Baron. But I have the temperament of Lermontov. I even look a little like Lermontov.[24]

Chekhov's own homages to Lermontov in his short stories have been documented.[25] In a chronicle of Russian criticism of Chekhov, Charles Meister shows how many nineteenth- and early-twentieth-century Russian critics say his work is empty and destructive to the social obligations of the writer: "indifference and apathy, inhuman" (Mikhailovsky); "the poet of hopelessness" with a "willful desire to 'destroy' his characters" (Shestov); a "prophet of nonexistence," "emotionally and spiritually empty" (Gippius).[26] These descriptions seem remarkably apt in describing the character of Solyony as much as that of Chekhov's art. The point is that the Solyony position in the world of *The Three Sisters* is a position recognized by those Russian critics as that of the socially irresponsible observer who is akin more to the romantic hero than to the social critic. But that irresponsible artist is also a character type that is found throughout in Russian literature. Solyony is a close relation to Pechorin, the hero of Lermontov's novel, *A Hero of Our Time*.[27] Solyony plays the role of Pechorin, whose goal is to be the hero of a novel. Both stand at an ironic distance from their social worlds and have the notion that the only action possible from such a position is destruction. From Pechorin's journal in *A Hero of Our Time*: "To be to somebody the cause of sufferings and joys, without having any positive right to it—is this not the sweetest possible nourishment for our pride? And what is happiness? Sated pride. . . . Evil begets evil: the first ache gives us an idea of the pleasure of tormenting another."[28]

To the extent that he performs the role of Pechorin, in other words, Solyony conforms both to that model and to the expectations of other characters in the play ("You impossibly dreadful man"). His action in the play is double faced: looking in one direction toward his modeled role and in the other at the characters around him. He is distinguished thus not simply by his ironic position but by the fact that he is not caught up by the paralyzing force of nostalgia. He is an intertextual character. Like Fedotik, he plays between the present material world and the imaginary, fictional one of a prewritten character—that is, in the realm of representation. But he also demonstrates the negative and destructive power of that realm. Unlike the sisters, he can act and move, but his action is to destroy. He may usefully break down the illusionary consciousness that prevents action and maintains itself in a nostalgic consciousness of loss and desire, but he leaves nothing in its place.

Both Solyony and Fedotik represent what the play in performance does in the world: it destroys the unitary forms of identity in games of representation. Such characters might even be seen as a Chekhovian habit if Charlotta of *The Cherry Orchard* is included among them. Charlotta, the governess who does magic tricks and acrobatics, also represents the alterative to nostalgia that binds characters in a stasis of nonaction. For Charlotta is performer, par excellence. Her actions as acrobat and ventriloquist are extraneous, redundant. She is a virtuoso of gesture and her heritage is the circus. In her self-description in act 2, which may or may not be melancholy, she says:

> I haven't got a real passport, I don't know how old I am, but it always seems to me that I'm quite young. When I was a little girl, my father and mother used to travel from one fair to another

giving performances—very good ones. And I did the *salto mortale* and all sorts of tricks. Then when Papa and Mama died, a German lady took me to live with her and began teaching me. Good. I grew up and became a governess. But where I come from and who I am—I do not know. . . . [*Takes a cucumber out of her pocket and eats it.*] I don't know anything. One wants so much to talk, but there isn't anyone to talk to. . . . I have no one.[29]

Having no self as defined by narrative, no clear origin, she is untied from an identity project and equally untied to either nostalgia for the past or hope for the future, with its attendant despair. Where other characters are representations of character, Charlotta is to some extent a nonrepresentational element who dresses as a clown, does card tricks, and somersaults. To be sure, in the speech above she marks her similarity with the isolation characteristic of Chekhov's characters. She is not a complete anomaly, but she does create a rift in the set of characters who guard their interior longing. She is exotic, relatively speaking, and puts the seriousness of the other characters into relief by opposing their constant conversation with performance activity (eating the cucumber; card tricks, ventriloquism; magic; cartwheels in act 3). In this sense she serves as Chekhov's own alienation device by throwing the represented world into relief through her playfulness. Charlotta is Chekhov's resistance to Stanislavski's sentimentality. Her presence iterates the performative elements of the events on stage, as does the shepherd playing the reed pipe in act 1, Yepikhodov playing the guitar in act 2, the Jewish band (or orchestra) playing in act 3, and the infamous breaking string in acts 2 and 4. Such sounds break through their narrative context like the acrobat and show the phenomenon of performance.

In their various ways, Charlotta, Fedotik, and Solyony are representations of a mode of action that is specifically not bound to the nostalgia or enclosed subjectivity that makes action impossible. They are significantly different from characters like Irina who are caught in the grammar of the imperative that makes the subject passive to the impersonal demand of the "must." Irina and her sisters are caught in the subjectivity that contains desire but cannot act upon it. The distinction between metaphysicians and performers is one between figures that seem to be psychological subjects—like "real people"—and figures who operate in the real time and place of the theatre. One—the idealized subject—is caught in a nonexistent reality that is immaterial and in a limited sense permanent. That representation can be recuperated in performance. But the other—the performer—is material and departs through the moments of performance in the ephemera of time.

The performers function in a pattern of appearances that is always partial, contingent, immediate. They play with and duplicate reality both in the sense of their own identity and the identifications of the world. Fedotik's photography equipment is technological playfulness that works over and against the singularity of the real, or what Derrida would call the metaphysics of presence. Fedotik's photos capture a moment by duplicating it, taking it out and away from itself: he makes representations that signify the moment. In that sense, the photo performs the real by its twin vehicles of multiplicity and duplicity. And it is these capacities to multiply, duplicate, and dissemble that inhabit performance and make it the antidote to metaphysical paralysis.

For comparison, it might be useful to consider Hamm's opening line in Beckett's *Endgame:* "Me to play." In that phrase, the subject has no intention. Any alteration in the grammar would falsify the position of the subject, so there are no equivalent formulations such as "I am playing; let's play; may I play; it's good to play." In keeping with the images of chess playing in *Endgame,* one might say it is Hamm's turn to play. His beginning, then, is not a willful assertion of intention but a response to conditions of a game. He simply announces his place in the rhythmic patterns of dialogue and narrative. But it is the pattern not the narrative goal that keeps him going. As S. E. Gontarski has put it with reference to Beckett's later plays, "an alternative arrangement or internal relationship . . . will emphasize *pattern* if not *order.*"[30] Order, presumably, would appear at the point where pattern conforms to a character's intent or desire; pattern appears where intent disappears.

In Beckett's theater, that is, the formal elements of rhythmic play rather than the ethical elements of drama constitute the action. This serves to obscure the dimensions of action that can be described as form and content, surface and depth, subject and object. In the language of desire and intention Hamm's speech acts appear to be disorderly and chaotic.[31] For what Hamm is doing throughout all these rudimentary dramatic deeds in *Endgame* is, as Ruby Cohn put it in the title of her book, "just play." As she writes in her introduction: "Beckett's plays are just play for precise performance. They are play as opposed to unmediated reality, but play is its own mode of reality."[32] To speak of Hamm as a representative of play, therefore, is not to limit Hamm to representation but to see how Beckett has been able to hold his drama at what one might call "zero-degree theater," where play is at once the mode and the representation in which speech and act coincide to an unusual degree.

Hamm's line initially suggests an antidote for Irina's problem in *The Three Sisters* whereby "Me to play" works in counterpoint to the imperative "We must work!" Indeed, Hamm might help solve the dilemmas of all those characters who exhibit the problem of how to act and who have difficulty in getting from one place to another, as I'll discuss them in the next chapter. Hamm does not speak of play as an intentional goal to be achieved but as a mode of activity in the here and now. It consists of expertise in delaying tactics. He wants, so to speak, precisely not to end, not to achieve, not to move from point A to point B, not to dwell in the metaphysics. "Enough, it's time it ended, in the shelter too. (*Pause.*) And yet I hesitate, I hesitate to . . . to end." He wants to resist achievement at almost any cost since achievement means the end of the game, although even to say he "wants" is to invest him with an intentionality that is not really evident. He resists the end because it would *be* the end. If Irina is stymied by the metaphysics and sublimity of "Moscow," Hamm would help her recognize that to achieve "Moscow" would be the end of everything.

Hamm is free of any metaphysical imperative. No ghostly father or weird sisters convene to suggest or compel his action or his achievement. He is also free of the dramatic order of action with its beginning, middle, and end. Play for Hamm is, in Reiner Schürmann's terms, a profoundly anarchic activity whose beginnings and ends are conspicuously marked as arbitrary. He begins by raising his "curtain," the handkerchief that covers his face, and his theatrical play begins by his becoming seen in spite of the fact he is unseeing, or at least in the dark. *Esse est percipi* (to be is to be perceived) is how Beckett begins his instructions for *Film*.[33] With the act of raising his handkerchief and announcing "Me to play," Hamm begins to "be there," to be perceived, and to play.

The lack of a proper narrative ending in *Endgame* reinforces this

idea. The play stops at a resting place in a tableau after Hamm replaces his handkerchief and is no longer seeing. Throughout, the
four figures have played like one of Beethoven's codas that will not
resolve to the tonic chord but will continue, as though improvised,
and keep on in spite of the demand from the unresolved sevenths to
finish. *Endgame* has the effect of having always gone on before. The
anarchy of the play is in its refusal to shape coherence out of cause
and effect determinants.

In beginning, in other words, Hamm is already given over to the
alternating play of turns and the structure of the game. "Me to play"
is as objective a statement as possible because it drains the subject of
indicative certainty, of willfulness, of intention, and of history as
well as futurity. He does not begin play, he is already in it. Hamm is
in the position of being played by the game he plays and thereby
combines the personal play of consciousness with the structure of the
game. In *Truth and Method* Gadamer puts it this way:

> Play is really limited to representing itself. Thus its mode of
> being is self-representation. . . . The self-representation of hu-
> man play depends . . . on behaviour which is tied to make-be-
> lieve goals of the game, but the "meaning" of the latter does not
> in fact depend on achieving these goals. Rather, in spending
> oneself on the task of the game, one is, in fact, playing oneself
> out. . . . Only because play is always representation is human
> play able to find the task of the game in representation itself.[34]

Play, in other words, engages representations, roles, masks, significations, and differences and works against an idealized, totalized, unitary sense of nature. Performance as play includes the notions that lead to its pejorative and its encomiastic uses: it's "just a
performance," done for the benefit of an audience, so by definition
it is false to nature. Fedotik's photos, like Solyony's adopted role,
are signifiers that set those characters apart from the interiority of
the family nostalgia that "maintains itself in a purely interior relation to itself."[35]

This is how play as performance is both the problem and the
solution for Hamlet the character. Throughout the play, of course,
Hamlet performs in the sense of pretending. That is to say, he is not
showing those hidden depths that "passeth show" to Gertrude,

Ophelia, Claudius, or Polonius; he is, rather, performing antic dispositions *for* them with the specific intent of concealing. In this sense,
the display of dispositions has the specific effect of showing one thing
that hides another: the play of representation and difference. The
chaotic exterior, of "doublet all unbrac'd," conceals both a further
chaos of thought and indecision and the more coherent darker purpose named revenge. What performance reveals in this instance is its
duplicity, not in the simple sense of dividing seeming and being, but
in the sense of multiplicity and radical variation. Just as Hamlet
shows himself to be effectively a different person for every character
he encounters and tends to reflect their own fears and expectations,
not unlike the play itself, his performing also carries the unifying
project of revenge.

Likewise, Solyony's variable, multiplicitous show of a melancholy disposition also destroys the unitary world of the sisters. This
sense of the performer's capacity for destruction is part of the anti-
theatrical prejudice that performance is dangerously destructive precisely because it does break down the idea of a transcendental unity
of the subject and the project. Performance, because it is a practice
rather than an idea, dissolves the idealized fixation of identity. Performance by its very multiplicity breaks down the singularity of an
authentic self—self that is at best only an idea that such a thing exists
apart from the field of play, which is the field of performing *for*.
Performing is a means of multiplying identities in the act of giving
away the singular self, just as Fedotik's photographs reproduce and
multiply Irina and the moment of his departure. The capacity for such
multiplicity is perhaps distinctive of human action. It works against
the stasis of nostalgia but also prohibits certainty. As Richard Griffith
put it,

> The putting on of appearances is our great and distinctive tal-
> ent. . . . I cannot expose my bare Being (perhaps even unto my-
> self), that is, make it appear without appearances; nothing could
> be seen. . . . As we study concealment and disclosure, depth and
> surface, the silence of the profound and the glitter of superfi-
> ciality—*of me embodied*—witnessing feign and fake, sham and lie,
> my veils and many masks, could it be that we will conclude that
> I am first and foremost: dissembler? at core a silkworm endlessly

concealing myself with what I am not, and that this concealing is my work of being?[36]

Performing, because it does involve adjustments to occasions and to being seen, brings action around full circle, from its source in the "person predicate" to the predication of the person upon the conditions of feigning, multiplying identities, and masking in the face of and because of others. Performance is wholly the social condition of being, such that even self-knowledge is dependent upon the capacity to mask, to feign, to pretend in the presence of the others. As Wilshire puts it:

> As one is authorized in his inauthenticity through manipulations of the other's recognition, so one is delivered from this state by allowing the other's recognition to manifest itself as it is. No manipulation is capable of freeing us entirely from the power of others; we can only further entangle ourselves by trying.[37]

The performer, then, is the ironist who is continually moving outside itself into new relational positions with others in the play of self-representation. It is constantly showing differences, dissembling, pretending to be other, and denying singularity. That motion makes the performer something like pure contingency or a pattern of appearances that appears as style rather than substance.

Play is crucial in terms of designating the attitude of an agent and the multiple as opposed to the unitary notions of action. But there are other ways to isolate the sense of performance and what I mean by qualities and style. For performance is a means of altering the perception of action as a substantive object with a set of attributes.

Within the closed space of the Prozorov world there are those characters who suggest alternative ways of acting that specifically avoid the paralysis of the imaginary. These characters are the pragmatists and the artists. Natasha, a pragmatist, is the outsider who marries into the Prozorov family. She breaks up the comforting world of the Prozorovs and gradually takes over the space. Like Lopakhin in *The Cherry Orchard*, who buys the orchard in order to save it, she is a realist. Chekhov's attitude toward such pragmatists appears to have modified between the plays, at least insofar as Lopakhin garners far more sympathy than the stupidly selfish and deceitful Natasha, whose excursions into the night with the unseen Protopopov are symptomatic of her betrayal and her success.

The three sisters, conversely, are engaged in a battle between the banality of contingencies and the spirit of hope, the battle that, in Chekhov's world, gives them grace, of a sort, and separates them from the brutality of Natasha, who fully accepts and is successful at dealing with the contingent world. The values of private kindnesses contrast thoroughly with Natasha's cruelty. Natasha enacts a brutal appropriation of territory that adheres to the power to do. But her capacity for action is combined with an inability even to conceive of a metaphysical ideal such as Moscow. In the Chekhovian character recipe, metaphysics are both the trap and the grace. The grace of the sisters is enacted in the treatment of the old servant and of the towns-people who lose their homes, or, by Ranevskaya in *The Cherry Orchard*, in squandering of the gold piece on a perpetually destitute neighbor. In other words, in spite of their inability to act in a conventional sense of fulfilling their intentions or desires, the sisters do perform in a qualitative way. Their small, contingent acts of kindness render them a quality of grace in such a way that one could say gracefulness *is* their action. They perform in small but actual gestures of kindness that are real, not metaphysical.

Natasha, conversely, has the capacity for action, for getting things done, for getting on with the future. She uproots the inactive characters, for all their goodness and their metaphysics. At the same time, she embodies a picture of human action that is bereft of both metaphysical possibilities and kindness. She demonstrates one version of what action is like when it is utterly free of a metaphysical imagination and is purely pragmatic in a worldly, problem-solving way. And what it is like is progress. What Lopakhin and Natasha demonstrate is that pragmatic action does indeed bring about change and the solution to certain specific problems; but because progress occurs in historical time, such progress can only be linear and such action can only be goal directed. Such pragmatic action has its costs in terms of kindness, in terms of the capacity of love and to dwell in the world gracefully. Pragmatic action has its trajectory and its directionality toward the future. Grace, unhappily, can neither save the orchard nor move the three sisters to Moscow.

What this suggests about the nature of action is that judgments and ethical evaluations that are so conventionally tied to the intentional structure of voluntary acts (*to act*) are not bound to that structure alone. Rather, ethical assessments are also founded upon qualities, which I outlined in the first chapter as the combined sensory and social gestures that constitute style. In a legalistic context, judgment is based on the motive of the agent. In such a context, loosely interpreted, we take note of the failure of the sisters' action to conform to their stated motives: to work or to go to Moscow. In a performative context, as I am delimiting it, judgment is determined in a separate code. While that code no doubt has cultural prejudices and signs, it is largely one of affective sense and pleasure. Kindness or grace, that is, are not motives: they are the affective products of specific gestures, like the donation of clothes to fire victims, the protection of the ancient nanny, and even the spoken longing for Moscow. In short, they are what the action as well as the nonaction of the three sisters feels like.

Grace, their performative element, constitutes their style but is not an inherently moral, immoral, ethical, or unethical act. It is not an object. Like happiness, it cannot be pursued, only derived. Yet it is why we (probably) *like* the three sisters more than we like Natasha, however much we may also be frustrated by their immobility. Such presumed liking may be at odds with other judgments. For, as *The Cherry Orchard* demonstrates, progress is a serious business, too serious to be left in the hands of the idle, if graceful, aristocrats who throw themselves and their orchard away.

The point here, in terms of the structure of action, is that the narrative or Oedipal form of the act, the one that correlates intentions and goals, is not the sole determinant of judgment. Nor is the performative dimension somehow free of judgments. It is simply of a different kind and order. The performative has its means of eliciting codes of value, codes that are even more illusive than those which attribute motives to agents, because they engage norms of feeling: pleasure or distaste, fear or approval. The performative code differentiates Fedotik's play from Solyony's. Performance may not take an act out of its volitional structure. One may well say that there is volition behind the care for old Anfisa. But performance adds the immediacy of sense and emotional response to the act.

The Three Sisters, that is, does precisely what the three sisters cannot do: it performs and completes an act by making it theater, that is to say, by turning it into a performance whose singularity is authoritative by virtue of being given through the time of a performance in a singular space where immediate responses count. The play itself, as a mask for its actors, multiplies and gives over its authority to the multiple experiences and interpretations and reactions of others. Its performance involves pragmatic contingencies. An actual performance plays between the ideality of the absent text, with its characters' roles, the sacrifice of that absent ideality, and the concreteness of time and space. The actual performance frames the absence without being consumed by it, like Fedotik's photos. Performance takes action out of ideal state and into the terms of actuality: play, masking, transience, impermanence, multiplicity, sacrifice to multiple interpretations and misinterpretation. At the same time, it pays homage to the *desire* for unity, singularity, and persistence. By insisting on holding out until the unitary ideal of action is immanent in the body's activities, Irina, Olga, and Masha will never work or get to Moscow, and yet by giving over their isolation to an audience, *The Three Sisters* converts their inaction to an act, placing it in the real world of contingency where props may fail, curtains fall, gunshots fail to go off, and actors forget their lines.

Chapter 5

How to Go about It

In by far the most famous of his soliloquies, Hamlet reasons against suicide. In that speech it is "dread" of the unknown consequences that "puzzles the will." To the degree that any action is a form of suicide because it eliminates possibilities, creates a past, and commits the actor to an identity, the reasoning may broadly serve to explain Hamlet's wider hesitations against action. To hold back means to keep possibilities open and to keep act and identity from becoming corpses.

> Thus conscience does make cowards of us all,
> And thus the native hue of resolution
> Is sicklied o'er with the pale cast of thought,
> And enterprises of great pitch and moment
> With this regard their currents turn awry
> And lose the name of action.
>
> (3.1.83–88)

The inhibitor against suicide here is less moral scruple than the dread that arises from thinking itself. Dread in the face of the gap between thinking and doing is attached to the void in the contemplation of death and belongs as much to mundane procrastination as to monumental deeds like murder. As Hamlet regards that void, there is no obvious site at which the mental act, which conceives both the completion of an act and the possibility of unknown consequences, transforms into a physical act. One formulation of Hamlet's difficulty, then, is how he can move from the interiority of thought to the exteriority of the body. From the outside, as an object put in view of the world, a subject is always acting out, or at least doing, something. But from the inside, from the position of a thinking, speaking subject, the gap between acting and not acting is immeasurable.

In the terms Hamlet has just given, his problem centers on the *name* of action. He cannot find the means or the time to join the noun that identifies the act (Revenge) to a verb (revenge). The further problem is how and when to insert his own name in the act. But why is there a distance between the noun and the verb, and what allows him to close that gap? The distance comes from the model of identity and action that conceives of the fully constituted subject that would exist prior to action, and from the reinforcement of this model in the division between nouns and verbs. The difficulty is in language, because of language. If language gives humans freedom from an inchoate presence, it also obstructs action by its idealizing capacities, particularly when it is the subject that idealizes itself.[1]

Gilbert Ryle insists that "when we describe a performance as intelligent, this does not entail the double operation of considering and executing."[2] The myth of intelligence is the myth of the "ghost in the machine" that supposedly gives the animating principle to a spirit, a spirit that is prior to operation. But that priority, or the notion of that priority, creates an infinite regress in which, he says, it would be impossible to begin an act. It replicates a mechanistic view of action arising from the Cartesian duality of mind and body. Ryle calls this a form of "occultism" that is a fundamental category error. For with the duality, it is impossible to explain how mind and body are ever coordinated. The mind is incapable of breaking through the ontological barrier to the body. This conceptual crisis constitutes a kind of motivational version of Zeno's paradox: intention could never reach achievement if the mind functions only in the realm of the spirit and is trapped in the body. But is this not just Hamlet's problem? Is he not trapped for four acts in the infinite regress of thought and the infinitive form of the verb, the form that is empty of person, place, tense, and time? It is the infinitive form the gravedigger has given in his analytic divisions: to act, to do, and to perform.

The mental regress for Hamlet lies in the problematic relation of subjectivity and language, a relation that is duplicated by the relationship of an actor to a text.[3] The name, like the text, places a demand upon the actor. The text provides a set of verbal instructions, and the performance carries out those instructions in the language of the stage, in design, image, gesture, and public time. Such is the commonsense view of the relation of text and performance. But in the name, or the text, the act is already determined, already has its identity. It is the conceptual artifact of a completed thing, a corpse that is dissected after the fact. In practical terms, it is already done, and how does one perform what is already finished? At what point can a subject leave language to do the deed? The name has no body, no contingency, no particularity. It escapes real time and is free of the contingencies of the present. Like a text, the name of the act offers a release from the uncertainties and unintelligibility of present action, but it is also incorporeal.

The name of the act is thus a symbolic identity for the sedimentation of gestures, rules, or conventions whose relationship has already been selected out from an inchoate world. It identifies a system of social forms. The revenge convention, for example, has requirements: an original crime; a call to reciprocate in kind from the ghost of the crime; a period of delay; a mask of madness and dissimulation. All these requirements along with the textual specifics of *Hamlet* participate in the name *Revenge*.[4] It is left over from the past in the form of institutional values, the Law of the Father, of myth and history, in the corpses of texts, all of which haunt the behavior of the living. It haunts social and theatrical conventions, providing models for actions, like Revenge, that have textual and social histories. The name of the act, like the Law of the Father, like the text, authorizes behavior and performance, but it also establishes constraints and inhibitions on behavior. At the level of abstraction and generality, it is devoid of particularity but enters the scene demanding to be enacted and to become corporeal. The ghost of the act haunts the living and demands revenge for its departure from the world. The broader version of Hamlet's problem, then, is not simply to enact revenge but to move from the symbolic to the real and thereby to revenge or redeem the symbolic by means of the real. In doing so, Hamlet must explode the symbol with the particularity and contingencies of the body, to disintegrate the meaning of the symbol by the fact of doing. This means that he must give the ghost its bodily enactment and, in a phenomenal sense, make it appear. These general points about *Hamlet* are taken from James Calderwood's close analysis of the play in his book, *To Be and Not to Be: Negation and Metadrama in "Hamlet."* Following that analysis, I want to indicate how the play exhibits answers to the broader questions about action and consciousness that concern me throughout this book.

One way to see the relationship between an abstract idea and materiality is through the idea of action as repetition, in which any specific enactment is simultaneously irreducible, something uniquely itself, and in constant reference to a demand from something that is not present. In discussing repetition, Lacan follows Freud in insisting on an important difference between the reproduction of an original trauma and the act of repetition, which involves the resistance or even denial by the subject of an original trauma, particularly in the presence of another, the viewing analyst.[5] The commonsense notion of performance is as a reproduction or mimetic duplicate of an original. Using a psychoanalytic distinction, however, repetition is an event of forgetting in which an encounter with a real appears in the guise of chance or accident, so that the event appears as occurring for the first time.[6] In these terms, repetition involves a loss of memory and history, not a recovery.

This notion of repetition might be close to what Stanislavski was aiming at when he insisted his actors imagine that they were performing actions on stage as if for "the first time."[7] That is, they needed to forget the reality of having performed similar actions before and focus upon the reality of the radical singularity of *this time* of performance. And that is not a hypothetical condition but a real one, involving the double condition of both remembering and forgetting the text. It requires losing the name of action in order to act: forgetting the textual demand in order to fulfill it. This is a peculiarly liminal state for describing the reality of an action that is both symbolic and real, displaced and concrete. I want to locate this territory grammatically in terms of an adverb, the part of speech that operates between nouns and verbs, and is specifically qualitative.

In Ryle's terms, Hamlet must demonstrate the difference between knowing *what* and knowing *how*.[8] Almost all the conventional explanations for Hamlet's famous delay presume that if he could merely get his intentions in order the act would follow. This assumption appears behind the complaint that his state of mind is the cause of his inaction. As Olivier announced at the beginning of his filmed version, "This is the story of a man who could not make up his mind." But, as Harry Levin put it, "Hamlet's state of mind is one of those questions upon which all the doctors have disagreed."[9] For the state-of-mind question implies an essentialist notion of character whose identity is constituted internally prior to the execution of the act. That notion is inverted if character identity is seen as a by-product of doing, as opposed to being a source of intentions. Yet the essentialist notion is not merely an imposition upon a subject from the outside world: it also functions when the demand is internalized and the Other is incorporated as an always-already existing command, taking the forms of ghosts or nostalgia or texts or abstractions.

The major question for Hamlet and his critics is when and where his revenge act originates. It is a question of how to begin. When does the act begin if it is an endless cycle of repetition that does not simply reproduce an original but reforms that origin in the specific circumstances the present? At what point is the subject inserted into the cycle? What does it mean for Hamlet to begin the act of revenge?

To begin, Hamlet must in some way give birth not only to the act but to himself. In psychoanalytic terms, as well as in the plot of *Hamlet*, he begins in an act of mourning. And perhaps mourning is the closest approximation of the paradoxical origin for action that is determined by an already existing absence. Psychoanalytically, he is mourning for the lost object, represented by the absent phallus or the Name of the Father. From this perspective, his task through the play is to name himself, which in his case happens to be identical to the name of his father, and thus is really to rename himself in the same term as his father, "Hamlet." His project is to render authenticity to the name through his actions and to make the name, as Calderwood has pointed out, designate his own irreducible particularity and recollect the father.[10] The lost object will in fact be recovered symbolically—as a symbol—when he cries out at the grave, "this is I, Hamlet the Dane." Such mourning is a positive act based upon an absence, leading toward the creation of an identity as a symbol.[11] It entails not bridging the gap between thinking and doing, between Revenge and revenge, but leaping into that gap.

In terms that are certainly not psychoanalytic, Kenneth Burke says something similar:

> to study the nature of the term, *act*, one must select a prototype or paradigm of action. This prototype we find in the conception of a perfect or total act, such as the act of "the Creation." Examining this concept, we find that it is "magic," for it produces something out of nothing.[12]

Hamlet's problem is to create an identity out of nothing, out of an absence. Now there is a contradiction here. On the one hand, Hamlet is not out to create something out of nothing, because that something already exists in the name of the act, in the name of the figure, Hamlet, and in the shape of the text, *Hamlet;* so it appears that he simply has to do *that* thing. But that thing is a nothing, a ghost, an absent Other. At the same time, he has to traverse the distance between the act and its negation, nonrevenge, as though having to leap the gap between the being and nonbeing of the act. The nonact, that is, is infinite; it has no particularities or qualities besides otherness. So Hamlet is challenged to make the absent, abstract idea of the act concrete and particular, not to reproduce it but to do it *now.* This is one way of describing the process, then, of becoming conscious, or at least of consciousness assimilating the Other in the form of the Symbolic. What happens in the course of action of *Hamlet* is therapeutic in the sense that Hamlet's action in the theater does assimilate the Symbolic into the real. He moves from a category of conventions, Revenge, into a category of the ultimate particularity, his name, and into performance.

This process illustrates the double function of the name, as a real repetition and a substitution. As a substitute for the real, it serves to keep an agent from concrete materiality, but as repetition, it identifies a certain irreducibility in material reality. The name is tautological like the infinitive in that it summarizes both temporal and material dimensions, and it is performative. That is, it is self-identical and does not mean anything other than itself. This is particularly the case for proper names. James Calderwood points out the nature of the proper noun and its relation to Hamlet's difficulties.

> As a class, proper names are the linguistic ultimates—the verbal quarks and neutrinos—of particularizing, the point at which an existentialist reduction would have to stop, since it is at that point that meaning is stripped from words and we are left to confront sheer being. Thus Wittgenstein observed that "a name cannot be dissected any further by means of definition: it is a primitive sign"; and Gilbert Ryle adds that "dictionaries do not tell us what proper names mean—for the simple reason that they do not mean anything."[13]

The proper name of the play, shortened by convention, is *Hamlet*, corresponding to the featured character, Hamlet, and this unity suggests one kind of tautology between play, process, and character. But given the earlier discussion, the proper name might also be a basis for suggesting that the play in fact projects no further significance insofar as it is a self-identical thing, an act that acts the problem of the actant. The play, in other words, is already the solution to the problems it raises. It is an occasion and a temporal process *when* meaning occurs, but its tautological nature prevents us from speaking the truth of its meaning without speaking over a corpse. It is an instance, in other words, of the recursive relationship of to act, to do, and to perform. Hannah Arendt has put the issue this way:

> With word and deed we insert ourselves into the human world, and this insertion is like a second birth, in which we confirm and take upon ourselves the naked fact of our original physical appearance. This insertion is not forced upon us by necessity, like labor, and it is not prompted by utility, like work. . . . To act, in its most general sense, means to take an initiative, to begin . . . to set something into motion. . . . This beginning is not the same as the beginning of the world; it is not the beginning of something but of somebody, who is a beginner himself.[14]

Before continuing with *Hamlet*, it might be useful to look at a similar problem of beginning an act that is uncomplicated by the moral, cultural, or psychological overtones of revenge. It is an example of what the analytic philosopher would call a basic action in the sense that it is purely physical. It occurs in Beckett's *Waiting for Godot*. Pozzo, having stood to view Vladimir's offstage urinary difficulties, says, "I'd very much like to sit down, but I don't quite know how to go about it."[15]

This is an odd statement. How can he not know how? If this were a psychological sort of play that is formed on the premise that speech and psyches are untrustworthy, one might assume that he is demonstrating that he does not really want to sit at all, that his real desire is to stand, to demonstrate his power or to keep moving. There is no indication for such interiority, nor is there anything to suggest an ethical concern. It does not say that he does not know if he *should* sit down, indicating a moral dilemma about the rightness or the value of the action. How can a character, even an absurd character, not know how to sit? Is Pozzo merely mad? What is the problem here? Suppose, in the gravedigger's scheme of things, that the specific and basic problem is how to do in the sense of move—how to put the body in motion. Then, by extension, one problem is to figure how to correlate the mind or will and the body, how to join praxis and kinesis to kairos, or the opportune moment, how to do it *now*.

Pozzo knows what to do and even has the desire to do it, but is unable to move from standing to sitting. This moment of arrested action reflects the larger action of the play in which the hesitations of thought, particularly Vladimir's, present the questions of *why* and *how* to go on waiting. In the larger scheme of the play, the characters go on by killing time. It appears that something has intruded between desire and physical motion. In that moment, time becomes faceless, like an invisible demon. Pozzo is clearly stuck, but rather than calling it an intrusion of some *thing* between thought and motion, we might say that for Pozzo at this moment a void gapes between himself and the campstool, a void opening out of thought because of thought's own temporal gaps. We cannot know the content of his thinking, but it is not the content that inhibits him; it is thinking itself with its inability to answer the question of how, and its fundamental incompatibility with doing. The how to of an action can be answered as though it were a simple objective question. How do you do it? You "put one foot in front of the other"; or you "send certain neuromuscular messages from your brain to your foot." But these responses reside in essentially technical description that may be accurate and, at some point, useful, but will leave us in despair of an answer to the question of how to go about it. The answer to the question how requires more than technical or scientific description.[16]

Pozzo is in the position of assuming that theory precedes praxis. At this moment in the play, Pozzo is illustrating what, in a mechanistic view of things, might be called a breakdown of the machine and thus a failure of a mind-body correlation. On the other hand, he might just be proving Ryle's case, that the Cartesian, mechanistic occultism (the fundamental category mistake) can never account for a coordinated relation between mind and body. From this point of view, no matter how much Pozzo wanted or willed himself to move to the campstool, he could never get to it: a perfectly Cartesian dilemma.

Pozzo's problem, like Hamlet's, is marked by the difference between knowing *what* and knowing *how*. The latter specifically includes, according to the O.E.D., issues of manner, means, condition, purpose (as in "how did that happen?"); but also "by what name," "with what meaning," to what effect; it is further an adverb of "extent, degree and amount" as in "how much?" How calls for description or explanation of processes, as opposed to why, which is a call for an account of motives and causes, and what, which asks for the name. The how of action is the adverbial domain in which substantives break down into sensory appearances and codes of quality, not meaning. It is the domain for assessing things like skill, style, or beauty.[17] And style, as the French say, is the je ne sais quoi of the world. That is, it is perceptible but not knowable; it cannot be possessed as a datum of knowledge, but must be felt.

Relatively few dramatic texts concern themselves with the ontology of action. It is more common, historically, to focus on ethical conditions and to eliminate gaps between desire, motion, and time by presuming a coherence of these elements contained in the agency of character. From *Oedipus* onward the ontological and dramatistic problems of *how* are already solved as characters go about their business of *demonstrating* how. The style of a given dramatic act is determined by the conventions of theater in a given historical period but is rarely considered as an element of ontology. And yet it is the very specificity of textual, visible, and aural style that makes action perceptible and identifies it as historical, shifting, and real at the same time. That is, style—the how—is part of being and an element for recognition. It is a means of identifying differences between, say, Shakespeare and Beckett, who can easily be constructed to signify or mean similar things. Because of their styles, one would never confuse the two. That is, we recognize an author's acts by style more than significance.

The manner of the act in its material production (which would include textual production) dissolves the differences between a dramatic plot and a theatrical event. It elicits a combination of explanation and demonstration—a showing with a telling—at the level that Roland Barthes called the "third meaning" and in terms of what he elsewhere said is the "grain of the voice."[18] In other words, it would be possible to describe to Pozzo the mechanisms of sitting, but much easier to show him how to sit. And in showing him how it would be necessary to go beyond the mechanistic motion of sighting, walking, turning, bending knees; it would be necessary to put the act in play in order to give the act of sitting a kind of dimensionality that neither technicality nor intentionality alone can encompass.[19] Yet even showing him how would not result in reproduction of my own sitting, since the particularities of any given Pozzo-actor would exhibit an utterly unique quality or grain.[20]

In the course of *Hamlet* we witness, at least textually, Hamlet's playfulness, though a specific production that may have a very different quality. What looks like deferral in retrospect becomes evidence that he has been performing all along. His antic disposition is in fact the means by which he is taking revenge throughout. It satisfies the conventions that the name Revenge demands, but it is a disposition that is not without doubts and those doubts constitute his strain. A crucial change occurs when he hears of the exploits of Fortinbras in Poland, where Fortinbras is going to risk thousands of lives for a worthless plot of land:

> Exposing what is mortal and unsure
> To all that fortune, death and danger dare,
> Even for an eggshell.
>
> (4.4.51–53)

Fortinbras provides a model not just as a man of action but as one who will risk all for nothing, who is thus a genuine player in a game that signifies nothing. After this, Hamlet resolves, "O, from this time forth, / My thoughts be bloody, or be nothing worth!" (4.4.65–66). This is a resolve to make thought corporeal but it is also a resolve to throw himself into corporeal, bloody play and to leave his doubts behind, like Macbeth. And here Hamlet leaves the scene for the rest of the act. It is a period for the actor and character to relax, and when Hamlet returns to the scene, he is at ease. The strain of his mind against action relaxes and he is fully in the game:

> we defy augury. There is special providence in the fall of a spar-
> row. If it be now, 'tis not to come; if it be not to come, it will be

now; if it be not now, yet it will come. The readiness is all. (5.2.208–11)

His readiness is equivalent to the athlete who is fully "in the game," who like the baseball pitcher or the jazz musician, is in a zone, and has found the rhythm. As a recent basketball hero said, "I felt like I got in a rhythm and I didn't feel anybody could stop me . . . I wanted to get it all out."[21] Hamlet's readiness is not preparation but presence. And he is ready to "get it all out," like an athlete. That is: he is ready to exhaust identity in action; to unname *Hamlet* and to rename it Hamlet, who will return eventually as *Hamlet*. Action and identity, in the speech above, are articulated not as things but as an attitude, breaking down conceptual definitions of the act and allowing the temporal paradoxes of past, present, and future to play fully in the perception. Readiness is the presence of consciousness in the present. But further, it is also an opening of consciousness toward the future without any attempt to leap out of the present into the past or future or the idea of the act. Thus it has the aspect of openness that is passive.

Now Hamlet clearly functions for most of the play with a witty style: it is a style that attaches itself equally to the action of speaking and thinking and killing. Hamlet introduces himself wittily, opening his character with a joke ("A little more than kin and less than kind"). And Hamlet acts likewise through four acts of the play, producing a character that is almost purely playful because it is not engaged in specifically corporeal action. Wit is the style of the mind of Hamlet that disengages him and allows him the free play through an enormous range of rhetorical digressions and elaboration that serve to defer as well as create an act. It is a style that allows a Hamlet to be almost comic.

The plot of the play follows this technique of digression in an almost endless series of deferrals and indirections that continually seem to resist forward action. The plot is as witty as Hamlet because its structure follows the forms of rhetorical argument rather than dramatic action, as Calderwood has illustrated:

In retrospect we can see that the form of the play, so stressed by Shakespeare, can be likened to several rhetorical constructions—what Puttenham calls "tmesis," "parenthesis," and "parabasis."[22]

The free play of the structure is thus kin to the mind—which is to say, rhetoric—of Hamlet. Such kinship gives the play itself a form of subjectivity that appears to be self-creating or, rather, self-speaking. The play, in this sense, is a subject, not an object, because it is a form of speech. But like Beckett's *Not I*, it is also a continual deferral against naming the subject. Tautologically speaking, the play is a subject in play *and* an object that is played. Character, furthermore, is a means of locating the subjectivity that is in play through the course of action. This is just to say, as Marion Trousdale has suggested, that character is a rhetorical place rather than the simple representation of a person.[23] But more than that, the character Hamlet locates qualities of consciousness in the action that are made particular by the actor. The trouble that Hamlet and the Hamlet actor have in acting highlights the trouble that consciousness has in the material dimension of action. Yet all the same, he is at every moment performing his act of revenge. For in spite of his resistance, the plot, like time, is moving forward. Or as John Lennon put it, "Life is what happens while you're busy doing other things."

After the murder of Polonius, the witty Hamlet disappears and the witting Hamlet returns. One may say that the witty style has kept Hamlet from engagement in action, but it has also been his manner of presentation: his how. After his exile, he returns in the mode of understanding. His language then changes style. He reports to Horatio how it happened that he found the letters ordering his own death: chance has intervened. The discovery of those letters is something that happened to Hamlet through no will of his own; the discovery required no self-assertion. It is as though the problem of intentionality is no longer a problem because chance, opportunity, and intention occur at the same time. He is no longer caught in having to organize intentions prior to action. Rather, his intent is simultaneous to his fate, much like Kenneth Burke's tragic hero who suddenly wills his fall in the act of falling. The providential suddenly conforms with the intentional, as it does for Macbeth, and Nietzsche's idea of willing one's own "fortuitous existence" comes into play. Likewise, plot and intention coincide as an event, shaping the action even while they appear to be conditioned upon accident. Barthes might have called these moments of "zero degree action." In Hamlet's case, accident appears as the shaping divinity:

           Rashly,
And praised be rashness for it—let us know,
Our indiscretion sometime serves us well
When our deep plots do pall, and that should learn us
There's a divinity that shapes our ends,
Rough-hew them how we will—

                           (5.2.6–11)

One way of describing this might be to say that Hamlet's consciousness has joined the same temporality as his fate. But in joining it, there is a curious absence of style in his character. Hamlet has relinquished the wit and autonomy of the earlier scenes and appears, in his absence, to have submitted to the action of the game. He is carried, as it were, by the flow of time but is carried in the mode of understanding. But he further represents the consciousness that wins understanding within the action.

The idea of fatality need not depend on a notion of some divinity that directs action from on high. It might better be understood as the limits of the game in which rules contain the action but do not dictate how the game is played out: that is left to the combination of chance and skill. The fatality game enacts its own laws that are played through by players. This is not unlike Gadamer's idea of play as a *mode* of being and action into which a player throws himself. It is also a model for hermeneutic understanding. In these terms, Hamlet is the subjectivity that plays *Hamlet* and who is taken by the nature of play itself. Hamlet's absence from the stage is the structural equivalent to the loss of self that Gadamer mentions:

the primacy of play over consciousness of the player is fundamentally acknowledged. . . . Play obviously represents an order in which the to-and-fro motion of play follows of itself. It is part of play that the movement is not only without goal or purpose but also without effort. It happens, as it were, by itself. The ease of play, which naturally does not mean that there is any real absence of effort, but phenomenologically refers only to the absence of strain, is experienced subjectively as relaxation.[24]

The analytic model of action that divides motive, behavior, and performance allows the problem of sequence to intrude and fear of futurity to hinder it. The assumption of prior intentionality becomes the kind of self-consciousness that inhibits action. In play, however, the act of playing creates the completed subject that is identified in retrospect. The agent does not determine the action but finds himself in the action. In the most extreme formulation of the tautology of action, *Hamlet* hamlets Hamlet. But equally, Hamlet hamlets *Hamlet*.

Plot is the evidence of the fatality of the game. Separate from intention and social context, it is a mechanism that operates like a physics or kinesis of motion, demonstrating the laws of necessity that only in imagination could have been otherwise. Hamlet puts his happy accident of discovering the warrant for his death in providential terms. Even in happening to have his father's signet ring to seal the warrant "was heaven ordinant." But this notion of Providence could also be described by Gadamer's notion of play: Hamlet has finally submitted to the sphere of play and a game whose rules do indeed shape the ends of the play. Even in the contemplation of death at the graveside, there is in Hamlet a kind of buoyancy that Gadamer describes as a feature of one who is possessed by the game, because buoyancy is a feature of the playing itself. Put in other terms, his character is no longer autonomously intending, but becomes part of the economic system of revenge. For revenge in particular is an economic act: it predicates harm or injury on a *prior* injury and is specifically a *re*payment. And Hamlet is played out by the rules of the game that constitute the economy.

This is also a way of allowing that Hamlet's act of revenge need not be considered in moralistic terms, but in responsive ones. Hamlet cannot begin the act of revenge as an autonomous agent who begins at a point in time, since the economics of a crime are already in place, are beyond him, or outside him, coming toward him from the call of an inhuman figure, the ghost. He can only respond or not respond to the demand. He might justify that response morally or rationally, as many of his critics have done, but the demand itself has nothing to do with a metaphysical truth. Revenge is a system that Hamlet occupies and as a system it takes him along within it. That it is a system outside the realm of human action yet making demands on the human is shown in the traditions and conventions of revenge that go back to the Greeks with the Furies, and to Seneca with his ghosts. That these figures are later translated into psychoanalytic terms in the figure of the Other illustrates the persistence of the sense that the demands in the psychic economy are also felt as inhuman, other, or unconscious and gradually become conscious in terms of the interplay, in Lacan's terms, between the Symbolic, the Imaginary, and the Real. The figure of Hamlet, then, can be seen as an intersection of these dimensions. He represents the way that the biological human is inscribed by the symbols of language that constitute a world, a linguistic world that differs from things. Hamlet is called on to negotiate those differences by taking a part in balancing them. This means, however, that as an agent, he can never be at the beginning; he can only join or not join.[25] Character, however, is no longer the essential origin of the action but evidence of a response to a world of existing conditions and situations. Character maintains a double sense here as both an imprint of characteristics, or what I have been calling qualities, and an ethical site.

"Whoever 'tries,'" says Gadamer, "is in fact the one who is tried. The real subject of the game . . . is not the player, but instead the game itself. The game is what holds the player in its spell, draws him into play, and keeps him there."[26] The plot itself is thus what animates Hamlet and shapes his ends: the *psyche* and the *telos* of consciousness in action. Hamlet, the consummate player, is mastered by the game that is represented by plot, but he is mastered with full understanding. And *Hamlet* enacts the unity of praxis, kinesis, and kairos.

Finally, of course, Hamlet and *Hamlet* perform, which is to say initially that they follow through on their intentions and find completion of the deed in the context of an audience. For the performance dimension of the Hamlet-act asks us to look at the context in which action occurs. In the most specific way, performance implies the need for an audience or observer to the action. But this does not mean that performance is simply the culmination or consequence of some previous process or exercise in motive gathering. Performance is not a result or a goal but rather the completion of an act in the oxymoron of ephemeral infinity that is the now. For performance is the occasion of the action where an audience (or consciousness) participates with the performer in a radical immediacy. It is the occasion for a circulation of the act between its various dimensions. But it is also an occasion for committing "what is mortal and unsure / To all that fortune, death and danger dare, / Even for an eggshell." The theatrical relation between performer and audience, thus, is a mutual leap into the void of meaning and the play of style.

Certainly by the time Hamlet actually stabs and poisons Claudius in his double dose of revenge, he has the full court for his audience. We might enlarge the sphere of performance, however, to include not simply witnesses to the act but to indicate the requirement of the appropriate context for the act. And context includes the theatrical concreteness of time and place. Hamlet cannot perform his act until he finds himself in the right theater, which is to say, in part, in the right place at the right time. Regardless of behavior or motive, the act is not complete until it is put into the theater. "Call the noblest audience," says Fortinbras at the end.

But this is where the play comes out from the void and where Horatio comes in. Horatio needs neither to conceive action nor to act, nor does he have any particular motive. But as friend and confidant he will bring the infinitive forms of Hamlet's verbs to the indicative mood, albeit past tense, and tell the "occurents, more and less" as well as the motives "which have solicited."

> But let this same be presently performed
> Even while men's minds are wild, lest more mischance
> On plots and errors happen.
>
> (5.2.393–95)

What is about to be performed by Horatio is what has just been performed for an audience. Futurity as well as past inhabit the present of performance.

Horatio has been Hamlet's perfect audience who will make known what has happened. He is there to redeem Hamlet's name—and the name of action—by telling his story. So with the recognition of the need for audience and storyteller, *Hamlet* returns the idea of behavior as the observable element of action. Behavior is unknown without the observer who perceives and creates pattern out of inchoate gestures or deeds, without the coronor who passes judgment. To make behavior known is to bring it into the sphere of the intelligible; but such intelligibility is at the cost of living and being. The story is a necessary fiction that severs the irretrievable moment of an action from the flow of time, yet redeems it by making it repeatable.

In an important way, Horatio gives birth to *Hamlet* at the point at which he says, "let this same be presently performed." He articulates recursive interplay between the stable, completed act and performance in which an audience is engaged. He promises to give Hamlet the identity of *Hamlet* as an act in the world. This is in fact the second birth mentioned by Arendt, the birth out of word and deed, the birth out of language that is not nothing but is always already at play in the economy of the world.

> You that look pale, and tremble at this chance,
> That are but mutes or audience to this act,
> Had I but time—as this fell sergeant, Death,
> Is strict in his arrest—O I could tell you—
> But let it be. Horatio, I am dead,
> Thou livest. Report me and my cause aright
> To the unsatisfied.
>
> (5.2.334–39)

Hamlet begins to show himself by naming himself when he leaps into Ophelia's grave and shouts "This is I, Hamlet the Dane." That moment in the play marks the point at which his acting, doing, and performing are synthesized: the action has a name, a material, visible gesture, and an attitude directed toward an audience. For up until then, his performance has been in the form of a negative and non-identity, an act deferred by wit.[27] He gives birth to himself within the void of the grave, of the Other. Up until that point in the play he has operated over and above the gap between thinking and doing. That is, he has suffered from the name of the act and its difference from motion. His first articulated desire ("O that this too too sullied [or solid] flesh would melt, / Thaw and resolve itself into a dew") is to be relieved of the burden and pollution (solid or sullied) of materiality that is the necessary physical agency for action.

Hamlet, like *Hamlet*, bears the burden of materiality, but it is that very matter that the ghost requires for revenge; spirit alone is incapable of concrete action. Hamlet is further aware that the motive and cue for action are somehow insufficient. As long as one can isolate the motive and the cue from the deed, as long as they are visible as separate entities, the action cannot be fully constituted. Hamlet has plenty of models to imitate, if imitation were all that were required for action. Fortinbras and Laertes demonstrate what to do and even how to do it. But to tell Hamlet to imitate them is equivalent to telling Pozzo to put one foot in front of another to get back to his campstool or to showing Hamlet a revenge manual. It is not the physical act alone, nor the observable deed nor even the convention that comprises action, but their combination. The act is as much the audience's as it is Hamlet's; together they make up a full act of name, deed, and performance: something that is at once a fact, an openness to the future of interpretation and meaning, and a retrospection upon events that have already occurred. The action is at once tautological (closed) and discursive (open to interpretation).

Performance, in short, has a multiple character. It is both original, relating to its immediate context and audience, and repetitious. This is obviously not startling news, but it does help to keep the notion of act as intention from dominating both doing and performing; for the performance itself is the answer to how in distinction to what. The usefulness of the act, however, is to keep the performance from the belief that it is utterly original, or *only* original and originating, that it is completely new or has magically bridged an ontological gap between being and nonbeing. It forces performance into a context that recalls its status as repetition (but not reproduction). For performance does not begin, it repeats; it is not autonomous any more than the name of the act is. Or at least its beginning is not necessarily an absolute beginning but a conventional one: it begins when actors and audiences agree. The interplay between performing, doing, and the conceptual act keeps action from resting in a metaphysical category (like Revenge), a purely physical motion (being stabbed, drinking poison), or a merely conventional moment for actors and audiences (eight o'clock on a Saturday night).

But Pozzo has been left standing. How does he finally sit down? Pozzo needs, he says, an invitation. In order to help, Estragon begs him to be seated. After the conventions of polite exchange and a second invitation ("take a seat I beseech you, you'll get pneumonia") Pozzo is enormously relieved. The invitation provides his *cue*, which is the theatrical way of saying it provides the impulse for his motion from standing, to walking to the stool, to sitting. And the cue comes not from himself but from Estragon. It is not, in other words, self-generated but comes from a response to a simple, social grace. That cue initiates the motion not as an origin but as a social convention in which the form of graciousness—a strictly conventional linguistic display—is sufficient. It is a call from the world, articulated by another human.

The exchange of social clichés between Estragon and Pozzo suggest that change is not a profound process, but a simple one:

ESTRAGON: Here we go. Be seated, Sir, I beg of you.
POZZO: No no, I wouldn't think of it! (*Pause. Aside.*) Ask me again.
ESTRAGON: Come come, take a seat I beseech you, you'll get pneumonia.
POZZO: You really think so?
ESTRAGON: Why it's absolutely certain.
POZZO: No doubt you are right. (*He sits down.*) Done it again! (*Pause.*) Thank you, dear fellow. (*He consults his watch.*) But I must really be getting along, if I am to observe my schedule.[28]

The mutual acceptance of a fiction ("you'll get pneumonia") provides, we might suppose, a kind of belief, if not faith, in the possibility of a reason for action that then allows Pozzo to move. The impulse and the fiction get Pozzo out of the stasis of thought and pave over the regressive void of thought. More importantly, the cue for action provides the means of saying, "The time is now." It bridges the gap of thought by means of social convention, suggesting that it is impossible to discuss the ontology of action without its social dimension. Because of this call, Pozzo can perform. The cue is the public time that, like a conventional theatrical performance, identifies the moment for beginning. The curtain goes up at eight o'clock: that is how we know to begin the play. It sets a public demand upon the performer to relieve the responsibilities of deciding when to begin. The cue affords Pozzo relief from the effort of willful self-assertion. For one of the problems of action is not what to do, but when to do it, and performance is that dimension which says when is now.

This indicates, moreover, the social character of time. This problem of when to begin is not simply psychological but a problem of being in time which is also a problem of being in the social world. For although it is possible to resist the conventions and social contracts of time, resistance alone does not overcome time either in the fact of the biological clock or the fact that the social world will continue in spite of resistance by individuals. It is *possible* to procrastinate and hesitate because it is possible for consciousness to refuse participation in time. The differences between that social time and the deferred time of discourse accounts for the fact that, in my experience, it is easier to show up for a performance than, say, to get a paper in on time. Language and writing can endlessly defer the now. But as *Godot* makes clear, the point is that time goes on anyway, in spite of the refusals and disavowals of consciousness. In Hamlet's terms, or the writer's, Pozzo is not ready. But when Estragon offers him an invitation and a social fiction, he seems suddenly to know how, because he does sit down.

In *Being and Time,* Heidegger writes about the public nature of now. "The 'now' which anyone expresses is always said in the publicness of Being-in-the-world with one another."[29] The public nature of performance (even if it is a private one—something done alone) is equivalent to the kind of social contract that creates a sense of now. Although it is not something Heidegger would say, it is possible to move within and between different qualities of time—say, between the atemporal, the sequential, and the now—but even those qualities do not exist as independent entities, or entities independent of, prior or posterior to, action, movement, and performance. In moving and doing, beings generate time all the while they are being generated and destroyed by it. And drama, again, is the art form that likewise generates and is generated by what Beckett in *Proust* calls the double-headed temporal monster, time. The actual or what he might call the "factical" aspect of now is its public, social character. The fact that we can agree on now without having to designate it suggests that now is generated primarily by agreement or convention, not by some objective character. By moving into that now we move away from the private consciousness of self and into the public contracts of motion, doings, and deeds in time, which nevertheless defy representation. Put another way, one moves from the temporality of mythos to the temporality of praxis. Again, because drama can employ multiple temporalities it is the form that demonstrates the complex interplay of times: now, then, yesterday, tomorrow, forever.

It is tempting to consider time as a sort of an invisible but substantive object, the raw material or substance out of which we construct lives and dramas, prefigured by our sense of practical action. But perhaps it is useful to resist temptation and see time not as the raw material but as the product of actions and thus of consciousness, physical motions, and performances. And just as there can be different kinds and qualities of actions there can be different kinds and qualities of time, depending upon the configuration of the act, the quality of consciousness that is engaged, and the conditions or the historical moment of understanding and reception. Kronos and kairos, in other words, are not out there waiting apart from the human ability to conceive them, yet neither are they simply imaginary.[30] They are in the human faces of the actors.

The moment of change from the atemporality of Pozzo's infinite regress into the directional or sequential time of motion-toward-an-object is, in fact, precisely dramatized by Beckett. A moment before his line, Pozzo has had a lyrical interlude. Vladimir has just returned from offstage, kicked over the stool, then "halts, straightens the stool, comes and goes, calmer." Pozzo says, "He subsides. (*Looking round.*) Indeed all subsides. A great calm descends. (*Raising his hand.*) Listen! Pan sleeps." Vladimir wonders, "Will night never come?" then *"all three look at the sky."*[31] The evocation of Pan, the momentary calm, the silence as all three look at the sky, watch, and wait: it would be easy to call this a Beckettian sort of pastoral moment, a stillness amid the agitation, a moment of deeper atemporality than even the inaction of the play as a whole. If we allow at least for its lyrical qualities, then another way of describing the moment would be to say that Pozzo is having difficulty shifting from the lyric to the dramatic mode, from the private silence and its attendant infinity to the public action and its imperative of now, which ends silence, privacy, and thought and generates movement.

Pozzo has been caught in the stasis of an attitude which, in Burke's terms, constitutes both a "pre-act" and its teleology:

> the wavering distinction between the attitude as preparation for action and the attitude as substitution for action, involves a similarly wavering distinction between the dramatic and the lyrical. If Aristotle's world is essentially a dramatic one, his God . . . is essentially lyrical. From the dramatic point of view, the moment of arrest that characterizes the attitude is a kind of "pre-act." But the lyrical attitude is rather the kind of rest that is the summation or culmination of action, transcending over action by *symbolically* encompassing its end.[32]

At this moment in the play, all the characters are *almost* finished, but that almost constitutes the nonlocal point between rest and motion. Again, the adverb lies between the states of being. Once Pozzo is able to move *at all* he is able to keep moving, to get along because, in a sense, he is carried by now and by the public, sequential nows that constitute the projection of time ahead of itself. The exchange of social politenesses, in brief, has thrown Pozzo into the motion. For Vladimir, however, not having engaged in that social intercourse, "Time has stopped." But Pozzo cuddles his watch to his ear and says, "Don't you believe it." And they go on.

The recursive relation of performance, physical activity, and the name of the act reinforces Mead's notion of a self arising from a conversation among social gestures, suggesting a recursive structure of temporal dimensions as well. It also implies that the act and the subject are not created from nothing at a beginning point in time; the model of a gap between act and nonact, how and how not, is in fact only a conceptual model, not an actual one. For in actuality, the act has already begun. Change might be measured, then, not by the difference between something and nothing but by the sense of *increase* in character or identity. What Hamlet needs to overcome is not a failed intentionality but the *idea* of the act as an already completed object that would implicate him exclusively in already completed identity. Hamlet's burden is not simply to revenge his father but to develop, as in a photographic metaphor, from the negative, "I have that within which passeth show," to something that *shows*.

To perform, then, is more than a further definition of do and act. *How* Hamlet came to be able to conform motive and action remains a mystery to rational thought. Yet an audience already knows how because it has been witness to the qualities of the action, whether those were of Olivier's Scandinavian melancholic, Mel Gibson's brash boy, or Nicol Williamson's neurotic. The audience knows, that is, just when it happened because it was there, but it may not be able precisely to define what. The act finds completion in a performance that includes not simply the killing of the king but the production of the play, *Hamlet*, with the face and body of Olivier, Gibson, or the anonymous student actor. In performance the name that substitutes—the text, or the Law of the Father—becomes simultaneous with the name that is existentially irreducible: *Hamlet* becomes Hamlet. It is not just that *Hamlet* refers to Hamlet, but that the dramatic action performs for us the three branches of the problem of action as well as its tautological nature.

Hamlet presents the end of the strain of the individual consciousness against the problem of action as an end of the strain of language against experience. Hamlet the character ceases to ask how action is possible, how to join consciousness with behavior, how to align motive, behavior, and performance, because he is performing, not merely intending. The poetic desires that sought but never achieved a unity of language, identity, and action are, at the end of act 5, disconnected, discontinuous. Hamlet's own language becomes less discursive, less "poetic," less textual, the closer he gets to killing Claudius. In the duel, his language becomes almost expletive until he again withdraws himself from doing and speaks to Horatio. Even then, his dying sentence is cut off and "the rest is silence." Such silence is the final tautology of "it is": the linguistic ultimate of the name that cannot have meaning outside itself, yet is not without significance. Action that has been concealed by its own name is momentarily revealed to be enfolded in its tripartite existence. It is revealed in its nature as a symbolic double that cannot escape language or the theatrical arena of visibility, yet is not identical to them. While its meanings are endlessly negotiable, it is nonetheless bound to the terms of irreducible fact, public time, and historical convention. In being renamed, the act has lost its origin, and the tautology of silence meets the tautology of action where to act, to do, and to perform define each other through the work of the Hamlet actor. Yet action continues to circulate between its multiple dimensions as Hamlet re-plays the *Hamlet* game.

Notes

Introduction

1. Aristotle makes the distinction between motion and intention throughout his work, in his treatises on the soul, ethics, physics, and rhetoric.
   See, for example, *On the Soul*, in *The Complete Works of Aristotle*, ed.
   Jonathan Barnes, Bollingen Series, no. 71:2 (Princeton: Princeton University Press, 1984), 433a9–18. But even a non-Aristotelian like Jacques Lacan makes a case for the difference between mere behavior and action:
   "to our knowledge there is no other act but the human one. Why is an
   act not mere behavior? Let us concentrate, for example, on an act that is
   unambiguous, the act of cutting open one's belly in certain conditions. . . . Why do people do that? Because they think it annoys others,
   because in the structure, it is an act that is done in honour of something. . . . let us take note of this, that an act, a true act, always has an
   element of structure." Jacques Lacan, *The Four Fundamental Concepts of
   Psychoanalysis*, trans. Alan Sheridan, ed. Jacques-Alain Miller (New
   York: Norton, 1981), 50.
2. Emile Benveniste, *Problems in General Linguistics*, trans. Mary Elizabeth
   Meek, Miami Linguistics Series (Coral Gables: University of Miami Press,
   1971), 132. The quotation continues:

   These notions are not intrinsic properties of nature recorded in language;
   they are categories that have been formed in certain languages and projected onto nature. The distinction between process and object is recognized only by someone who starts with the classifications of his native
   language and then transposes them into universals; and this person himself, when questioned about the basis of this distinction, will quickly
   come to see that if "horse" is an object and "to run" is a process, it is
   because one is a noun and the other a verb. A definition that seeks a
   "natural" justification for the manner in which a particular idiom orga-
   nizes its notions is condemned to circularity. . . . In Hupa (Oregon), active or passive verbal forms in the third person are used as nouns: *nañya*
   'it comes down,' is the word for "rain"; *nilliñ* 'it flows,' designates
   "creek."

3. In *Truth and Method* Hans-Georg Gadamer uses play as a phenomenal category that can engage the opposition but does not rest at either extreme.

> Play is structure—this means that despite its dependence on being played it is a meaningful whole which can be repeatedly represented as such and the significance of which can be understood. But the structure is also play, because—despite this theoretical unity—it achieves its full being only each time it is played. It is the complementary nature of the two sides of the one thing that we seek to underline, as against the abstraction of aesthetic differentiation.

Gadamer, *Truth and Method*, trans., ed. Garrett Barden and John Cumming (New York: Crossroad, 1986), 105.

4. Wolfgang Iser, *The Fictive and the Imaginary: Charting Literary Anthropology* (Baltimore: Johns Hopkins University Press, 1993), 250.
5. See Martin Heidegger, *What Is Called Thinking?* trans. J. Glenn Gray (New York: Harper and Row, 1968). He notes that while "thinking is thinking *of*," the preposition *of* is equally divisive and unifying. By the same token, he indicates that thinking need not be found prior to physical acts, as though lying in wait for thought to be executed. "Every motion of the hand in every one of its works carries itself through the element of thinking, every bearing of the hand bears itself in that element. All the work of the hand is rooted in thinking" (16).
6. Bruce Wilshire, "Theatre as Phenomenology: The Disclosure of Historical Life," in *Phenomenology: Dialogues and Bridges,* ed. Ronald Bruzina and Bruce Wilshire (Albany: State University of New York Press, 1982), 357.
7. I am referring here to Gadamer's idea that play specifically involves a loss of self to the rules of the game. Volition and identity, that is, are taken over by the game. This is not to say a player may or may not choose to play, only that "The attraction of a game, the fascination it exerts, consists precisely in the fact that the game tends to master the players . . . . Whoever 'tries' is in fact the one who is tried. The real subject of the game . . . is not the player but the game itself." Gadamer, *Truth and Method*, 95–96.

Chapter 1

1. All quotations from *Hamlet* are from *The Riverside Shakespeare* (Boston: Houghton Mifflin, 1974).
2. Consider Arthur Danto, for example, discussing figures in a series of tableaux that portray Christ with an identical gesture. He recognizes that the meaning of any act or gesture—the raising of an arm—is inevitably contextual, but he is primarily interested to "isolate those bare, neutral actions before they are colored by the sort of meanings they are shown to have on the Arena walls and in common life." Arthur C. Danto,

Analytic Philosophy of Action (Cambridge: Cambridge University Press, 1973), ix.

3. The *actual* on stage, is, of course, a serious dilemma. In most productions, the gravedigger will be executing some actual set of motions that *count* as digging a grave within the conventional system or game of that production. The question of the reality of stage action and its logical foundation in the reality of a game is thoroughly examined by David Z. Saltz in "The Reality of the Theatre Event: Logical Foundations of Dramatic Performance" (Ph.D. diss., Stanford University, 1992).

4. A good number of productions bring back the "body" of Polonius by having the same actor play both parts in a move of efficient casting that further signals the similarity.

5. Harry Levin, *The Question of Hamlet* (Oxford: Oxford University Press, 1959), 79. How those changes resound specifically, he does not say. Joan Hartwig, by contrast, was willing to name the differences quite specifically.

"Acting" with its punning significance of the theatrical putting on of a role other than what the person is; "doing" with its ambivalent sexual and direct physical action implied; and "performing" with its adjustments according to the performer's sense of how the audience perceives him *are* distinct values of the "act."

Joan Hartwig, *Shakespeare's Analogical Scene* (Lincoln: University of Nebraska Press, 1983), 11–12.

6. In the *Nichomachean Ethics* and in the *Rhetoric* Aristotle raises the issues of assessing the responsibility of the agent, or "person predicates," for action. He explicitly divides voluntary from involuntary and compulsory actions. Although it seems self-defining, compulsory acts are those in which "the cause is in the external circumstances and the agent contributes nothing" (*Nichomachean Ethics* in *Complete Works*, 1110b1). In this realm, knowledge is everything, so that the voluntary is defined as "anything in a man's own power which he does with knowledge" (1135a16). Conscious choice—the process of deliberation—combined with "power" (meaning both capacity and opportunity), in other words, is the hallmark of just or right action. That is, involuntary acts are only incidentally just or unjust. The origin of the just act is choice: "and [the origin] . . . of choice is desire and reasoning with a view to an end. This is why choice cannot exist either without thought and intellect or without a moral state" (1139a33). In any case, the crucial issue is volition.

7. Paul Ricoeur, *Time and Narrative,* trans. Kathleen McLaughlin and David Pellauer (Chicago: University of Chicago Press, 1984), 1:55.

8. "Actions," says Ricoeur, "imply goals . . . which commit the one on whom the action depends. . . . Actions refer to motives. . . . Actions also have agents, who . . . can be held responsible for certain consequences of their actions. In this network, the infinite regression opened by the

question 'Why' is not incompatible with the finite regression opened by the question 'Who?'" Ricoeur, *Time and Narrative*, 1:55.

9. Bert O. States, *"Hamlet" and the Concept of Character* (Baltimore: Johns Hopkins University Press, 1992), 138.

10. The shape of such an act is described by Aristotle as both spatial and temporal in *On the Soul:*

These two at all events appear to be sources of movement: appetite and thought. . . . both of these then are capable of originating local movement: thought, that is, which calculates means to an end, i.e. practical thought (it differs from speculative thought in the character of its end): while appetite is in every form of it relative to an end; for that which is the object of appetite is the stimulant of practical thought; and that which is last in the process of thinking is the beginning of the action. (433a9–18).

11. The alignment of action and speech is hardly new. Structuralist poetics derive specifically from the idea that plot or narrative derives from grammatical rules of order. Those structuralist theories, particularly after Propp, aimed at giving a kind of scientific authority to the mechanics of plot and narrative. Grammar inhabits the narrative utterance as a system of possible relations. They attempt to codify and, as Thomas Pavel says, "to grasp the phenomenon of plot-advance, the simple and obvious fact that plots link together actions performed by the characters." Thomas G. Pavel, *The Poetics of Plot: The Case of English Renaissance Drama* (Minneapolis: University of Minnesota Press, 1985), 17. The poetics of narrative theory are founded in the notion that action unfolds like a sentence, with digression and elaboration, to be sure, but essentially toward an ending point. It is a measure of change from one point to another. The narrative act can be parsed, like a sentence, and is thus essentially linear, moving forward along a line of time. But the structuralist method rarely allows for the context of the narrative act itself and the complications that context and reception entail. Yet the narrative act creates the concepts of time. As Wlad Godzich puts it in the foreword to Pavel's book, "the ontological primacy of action renders the question [of whether time or causality is primary] moot and . . . one has to turn it around and see whether the articulation of action is not what gives us both our sense of temporality and of causality" (xxi–xxii).

12. Peter Brooks, *Reading for the Plot* (New York: Vintage, 1984), 22.

13. Teresa de Lauretis, "Snow on the Oedipal Stage" and "Desire in Narrative," in *Alice Doesn't: Feminism, Semiotics, Cinema* (Bloomington: Indiana University Press, 1982).

14. "The self to which we have been referring arises when the conversation of gestures is taken over into the conduct of the individual form. When this conversation of gestures can be taken over into the individual's con-

duct so that the attitude of the other forms can affect the organism, and the organism can reply with its corresponding gesture and thus arouse the attitude of the other in its own process, then a self arises." George Herbert Mead, *Mind, Self, and Society*, ed. Charles W. Morris (Chicago: University of Chicago Press, 1934), 1:167.

15. Mead, *Mind, Self, and Society*, 1:201.
16. Kenneth Burke, *A Grammar of Motives* (Berkeley and Los Angeles: University of California Press, 1969), 237.
17. Mead, *Mind, Self, and Society*, 1:255.
18. "A symbolic system thus furnishes a descriptive context for particular actions. In other words, it is 'as a function of' such a symbolic convention that we can interpret this gesture as meaning this or that. The same gesture of raising one's arm, depending on the context, may be understood as a way of greeting someone, of hailing a taxi, or of voting. Before being submitted to interpretation, symbols are interpretants internally related to some action.

    In this way, symbolism confers an initial *readability* on action." Ricoeur, *Time and Narrative*, 1:58.
19. Reiner Schürmann, *Heidegger on Being and Acting: From Principles to Anarchy* (Bloomington: Indiana University Press, 1987), 243.
20. This view of the symbolic force within cultural practices has been at the root of the change in anthropological research over the last quarter of the century. See especially Clifford Geertz, *Local Knowledge: Further Essays in Interpretive Anthropology* (New York: Basic Books, 1983) and *Works and Lives: The Anthropologist as Author* (Stanford: Stanford University Press, 1988).
21. Paul Ricoeur and Hans-Georg Gadamer, "The Conflict of Interpretations," in Bruzina and Wilshire, *Phenomenology*, 308.
22. Seymour Chatman, "What Novels Can Do That Films Can't (and Vice Versa)," *Critical Inquiry* 7, no.1 (autumn 1980): 128.
23. Charles Altieri, *Act and Quality: A Theory of Literary Meaning and Humanistic Understanding* (Amherst: University of Massachusetts Press, 1981), 102. Altieri quotes sec. 621 of the *Philosophical Investigations*.
24. Hayden White, "The Value of Narrativity in the Representation of Reality," *Critical Inquiry* 7, no.1 (autumn 1980): 11–12.
25. René Descartes, quoted in Jean-Claude Beaune, "The Classical Age of Automate: An Impressionistic Survey from the Sixteenth to the Nineteenth Century," in *Fragments for a History of the Human Body*, ed. Michel Feher, Ramona Naddaff, and Nadia Tazi (New York: Zone, 1989), 1:444.
26. Heinrich von Kleist, quoted in Roman Paska, "The Inanimate Incarnate," in Feher, Naddaff, and Tazi, *Fragments for a History*, 1:417.
27. Peter Handke, "Offending the Audience," in *Kaspar and Other Plays*, trans. Michael Roloff (New York: Grove, 1969), 21.
28. States, *Concept of Character*, 138–39.
29. Jacques Lacan, "The Signification of the Phallus," in *Écrits*, trans. Alan Sheridan (New York: Norton, 1977), 281–91.

30. Merleau-Ponty puts it this way: "As long as the body is defined in terms of existence-in-itself, it functions uniformly like a mechanism, and as long as the mind is defined in terms of pure existence-for-itself, it knows only the objects arrayed before it. The distinction between abstract and concrete movement is therefore not to be confused with that between body and consciousness; it does not belong to the same reflective dimension, but finds its place only in the behavioral dimension." Maurice Merleau-Ponty, *The Phenomenology of Perception,* trans. Colin Smith (London: Routledge, 1962), 124.

31. Josette Féral, "What Is Left of Performance Art? Autopsy of a Function; Birth of a Genre," *Discourse* 14, no.2 (spring 1992): 142–62.

32. When athletes are performing their skills, what becomes perceptible is skill or style. In some sense, in watching a baseball game or a tennis match, it is only style that one sees. Style actualizes the game, but the perceptible is not the game but qualities of play. Matches become interesting, for example, when players of similar styles contest each other: the match takes on very subtle deviations in a contest of styles. The athletic performance is indicative of performance in general because it demonstrates concretely the negotiation between the potentials or limitations of the athlete and the rules of the game. The performance fills the space between capacities and rules or situational demands. And it fills that space with qualities more than substance. Indeed the conventional division between style and substance accounts for the persistent belief that performance is merely show, hence pretense, hence false consciousness or bad faith. The show, rather, is identical to actuality.

33. Roland Barthes, *Image-Music-Text,* trans. Stephen Heath (New York: Hill and Wang, 1977), 54. Taking his example from some of Eisenstein's still shots for a notation of a meaning that is neither signification nor a mere fact of existence, Barthes says:

> I do not know what its signified is, at least I am unable to give it a name, but I can see clearly the traits, the signifying accidents of which this— consequently incomplete—sign is composed: a certain compactness of the courtiers' make-up, thick and insistent for the one, smooth and distinguished for the other; the former's "stupid" nose, the latter's finely traced eyebrows. . . . On the one hand, it cannot be conflated with the simple *existence* of the scene, it exceeds the copy of the referential motif, it compels an interrogative reading . . .; on the other, neither can it be conflated with the dramatic meaning of the episode: to say that these traits refer to a significant "attitude" of the courtiers, this one detached and bored, that one diligent. (53)

34. "This text [of bliss] is outside pleasure, outside criticism, *unless it is reached through another text of bliss:* you cannot speak 'on' such a text, you can only speak 'in' it, *in its fashion,* enter into a desperate plagiarism, hysterically affirm the void of bliss (and no longer obsessively repeat the

letter of pleasure.)" Roland Barthes, *The Pleasure of the Text*, trans. Richard Miller (New York: Hill and Wang, 1973), 22. Barthes has already distinguished this sense of bliss from the "Oedipal pleasure" of a text's "corporeal striptease or of narrative suspense . . . to denude, to know, to learn the origin and the end" (10). This would be the pleasure associated with the revelation of the act.

35. *Cognitive, rhetorical,* and *formal* are terms used by Wesley Trimpi to describe the "ancient hypothesis of fiction," which describes the threefold functions of literature. The categories overlap but encompass what he calls the "speculative (cognitive), the prudential (juridicative), and the productive (formal)" as operations of the disciplines of philosophy, rhetoric, and mathematics that serve respectively to transmit knowledge, to persuade, and to formalize experience. These likewise correspond to Plato's categories of the true, the good, and the beautiful. Trimpi sees the history of literary criticism as the history of correction of the imbalances in the emphasis of one function over the others. Wesley Trimpi, *Muses of One Mind: The Literary Analysis of Experience and Its Continuity* (Princeton: Princeton University Press, 1983).

Chapter 2

1. Samuel Beckett, *Waiting for Godot* (New York: Grove Press, 1954), 7.
2. Charles Altieri points out that among recent philosophers of action, almost all "agree roughly on the basic opposition which gives sense to the term *action:* a distinction between happenings which do not involve person predicates, and the sphere of actions where an event is in some sense qualified by the effects of an agent's wants or beliefs or reasons" (*Act and Quality*, 102). And of course, this fundamental distinction does not belong to recent philosophers alone: it begins, not surprisingly, with Aristotle. Human actions, as described in the *Nichomachean Ethics*, are differentiated from mere motion and changes manifest in nature. They are either voluntary or involuntary. The difference is determined primarily by the outcome. After distinguishing voluntary from involuntary or compulsory actions, Aristotle then differentiates involuntary from nonvoluntary. "Everything that is done by reason of ignorance is *non*-voluntary; it is only what produces pain and regret that is *in*voluntary" (1110b17). Then reasoning by contraries, he says, "Since that which is done under compulsion or by reason of ignorance is involuntary, the voluntary would seem to be that of which the moving principle is in the agent himself, he being aware of the particular circumstances of the action" (1111a21). In other words, in the broadest sense actions are thoroughly linked to human agents and by those human agents to a goal. The teleological notion of action begins here. Even more specifically, however, for Aristotelian ethics, human agents significantly define their characters by their acts within the sphere of the human community. So acts are not simply things in themselves. They are political just as character is politi-

cal. In the Aristotelian tradition the formation of an act is distinguished by a concept of a relation between intentions and deeds. Intention is the differential of an event and an act. For Aristotle, the difference between kinesis and praxis is the difference between purely physical and social or intentional acts. The stone that falls cannot will its fall, but does so spontaneously or incidentally in accordance with physical laws, not by choice. Volition is consonant with the act. But as the Estragon line indicates, there can be a dissonance between the volition and the construction of an act.

3. See, especially, W. J. T. Mitchell, ed., "On Narrative," special issue of *Critical Inquiry* 7, no.1 (autumn 1980); de Lauretis, *Alice Doesn't;* Maria Minich Brewer, "A Loosening of Tongues: From Narrative Economy to Women Writing," *MLN* (December 1984): 1141–61; Susan S. Lanser, "Toward a Feminist Narratology," *Style* 20 (fall 1986): 341–59.

4. Kenneth Burke, "On Piety," in *Permanence and Change* (Indianapolis: Bobbs-Merrill, 1965), 78.

5. The conceptual structure of volition itself generates its own past, its own narrativity, its own identity because it is a linear structure. The acting out of an intention is a means of turning a subject into its own object. In being predicated upon a previously existing subject, that is, the intentional act is already a narrative act. In Paul Ricoeur's description discussed in the last chapter, the conceptual network by which we understand narrative is a prefiguration involving a view that agents can be held responsible for their actions and consequences. This view of relations between deeds and agents is, he admits, already culturally mediated by signs and symbols that determine what a given act might *mean,* or what kinds of things one may or may not be held responsible for. But the point is that the structure of volition is Aristotelian and depends upon the agent's predating the act. To the degree that it implies a goal—to have the boot off—it is a notation for a set of relations by which an act is distinguishable from activity. But a willful assertion toward a future or a goal is not only linked to its own past: in a way it creates that past. Indeed, goal-directed activity is a means of understanding how in a sense, a past is generated.

Likewise, a narrative shape is a shape of knowledge. Such a premise informs the perspective of diverse narrative investigations from the structuralism of Propp and Roland Barthes to Sartre; Walter Benjamin's "The Storyteller: Reflections on the Works of Nikolai Leskov" in *Illuminations,* ed. Hannah Arendt, trans. Harry Zohn (New York: Schocken, 1969); Frank Kermode's *The Sense of an Ending* (New York: Oxford University Press, 1967); Ricoeur's *Time and Narrative;* and Brooks's *Reading for the Plot,* to name only a few. And what generates the sense of motion toward an end has been loosely called, by Brooks and others, "narrative desire." "Narratives," says Brooks, "both tell of desire . . . and arouse and make use of desire as dynamic of signification" (37).

6. See Paul Hernadi, "Doing, Making, Meaning: Toward a Theory of Verbal Practice," *PMLA* 103, no.5 (October 1988): 749–58. Hernadi takes writing, as I am taking action, to be a threefold activity, though with a different emphasis. In doing something, he says, one also makes something (an object) and means something. I would also say that Estragon means to take off his boot and cannot simply ignore that intentionality or purpose. But my focus here, in terms of Hernadi's categories, is on the making of a sense of substance for an act.

7. Peter Brooks in particular summarizes much of the narrative theory that deals with how what Frank Kermode called the sense of an ending serves to confer identity on action. Brooks describes the narrative drive toward death in specifically Freudian terms in the chapter "Freud's Masterplot" in *Reading for the Plot*. But the coherence of ends and beginnings as definitive of narrative certainly goes back to Oedipus (see also Barthes, *Pleasure of the Text*).

8. Georg Lukács, "The Sociology of Modern Drama," trans. Lee Baxandall, in *The Theory of the Modern Stage*, ed. Eric Bentley (Harmondsworth, England: Penguin, 1968), 429.

9. Anthony Kenny, *Action, Emotion, and Will* (London: Routledge and Kegan Paul, 1963), 178.

10. Kenny, *Action, Emotion, and Will*, 176.

11. Bruce Wilshire, *Role Playing and Identity: The Limits of Theatre as Metaphor* (Bloomington: Indiana University Press, 1982), 37. Wilshire takes Sartre's rearrangement of grammatic structure from subject/predicate and subject/object, also following on Vico:

> For Vico there is no primordial "given." What is primordial is formed— formed by imagining and perceiving bodies imagining concretely in the "imaginative universal." . . . After Vico, Sartre, for instance, can rearrange our descriptive schemata: instead of saying, for example, "I fear the gorilla," or "Fear is present in me as a subjective attribute of a substance," we can say, "The Fear gorillas me." It is difficult to overestimate the importance of this conceptual turn. (36–37)

12. To a great degree, Estragon's active/passive formula is a version of the "total act" discussed by Burke. The difference between Burke's version of the total act and the Aristotelian version of action is found in Burke's suggestion that the act serves to convert the actant. This is quite distinct from the notion that the actant is an instance of Aristotle's "unmoved mover." For the model of action to replicate an organic life cycle one must presume that a subject is fully constituted prior to its actions (the unmoved mover). The organic foundation gives the effect of a natural subject that is outside or beyond or free of language and the signifying processes through which both action and subjects are in fact constituted. For a life is not an act and the biological cycle is not a subject. Estragon's line, that is, does not suggest a *passage* from one state to another, as in

the past retreating from the present, but a simultaneity of active and passive, an end in the present. The sense of change from active to passive is reflected in Burke's important description of the "dialectic of tragedy," in which he points out how the tragic act is a simultaneous exertion and passion, deed and suffering.

> Stated broadly the dialectical (agonistic) approach to knowledge is through the *act* of assertion, whereby one "suffers" the kind of knowledge that is the reciprocal of his act. . . . It is deplorable but not tragic, simply to be a victim of circumstance, for there is an important distinction between destiny and sheer victimization.

Burke, *Grammar of Motives*, 38–39. The passage continues:

> Sheer victimization is not an assertion—and naturally makes not for vision but for frustration. The victimizing circumstances, or accidents, seem arbitrary and exorbitant, even "silly." But at the moment of tragic vision, the fatal accidents are felt to bear fully upon the act, while the act itself is felt to have summed up the character of the agent. Nor is this vision a sense of cosmic persecution; for in seeing the self in terms of the situation which the act has brought about, the agent transcends the self. (39)

13. Samuel Beckett, *Proust* (New York: Grove Press, 1957), 2.
14. This is the basis for Judith Butler's argument against any notion of a gendered subject that might acquire the attributes of gender through action as much as her argument against a substantive notion of gender that acquires adherents by kind of behavior. Butler argues that it is more complicated than the substantive/attributive model allows, and that gender is, rather, "performative." Her use of the word *performance* is not mine, but the idea that gender is a signifying and signified, that it is simultaneous with actions, is a negotiation with and against social meanings, and is therefore an unstable category describes in a specific way and with a specific term (gender) the dynamics of the subject and action that I want to describe more generally (though not more universally). See Judith Butler, *Gender Trouble: Feminism and the Subversion of Identity* (New York: Routledge, 1990).
15. In his essay, "The Schizophrenic and Language," Gilles Deleuze points out an important difference in the nonsense of the language of the poem "Jabberwocky" and the language of the schizophrenic by discussing Antonin Artaud's translation of Carroll's poem. Wishing to differentiate the language of the child, the schizophrenic, and the poet, each of whom may use nonsense language, including portmanteau words, Deleuze points out that Carroll's language is in effect a "mastery of the surface," while the schizophrenic discovers that "there is no more surface . . . bodies no longer have a surface. . . . As a result, the entire body

is nothing but depth." Gilles Deleuze, "The Schizophrenic and Language," in *Textual Strategies*, ed. and trans. Josué V. Harari (Ithaca, N.Y.: Cornell University Press, 1979), 286. The language that can master the surface might be something that linguistically indicates the simultaneity of lightning and flash; whereas the schizophrenic language might not simply persevere at the level of "lightning" but at the level at which the word itself occupies the surfaceless depth where "words become physical and affect the body immediately" (287).

16. Friedrich Nietzsche, *On the Genealogy of Morals*, trans. Walter Kaufmann (New York: Vintage, 1969), 45.

17. Michel Haar, "Nietzsche and Metaphysical Language," in *The New Nietzsche: Contemporary Styles of Interpretation*, ed. David Allison (New York: Delta, 1977), 18. I found this first cited in Butler, *Gender Trouble*, 20.

18. Ludwig Wittgenstein, *Philosophical Investigations*, trans. G. E. M. Anscombe (New York: Macmillan, 1953), sec. 621.

19. Through the construction of an act the boundaries of nonaction are also defined, and together they define both time and subjects. As Wlad Godzich puts it, "the ontological primacy of action renders the question [of whether time or causality is primary] moot and . . . one has to turn it around and see whether the articulation of action is not what gives us both our sense of temporality and of causality." The perception of causality, that is, occurs after the fact, after the act appears through language and narrative. Causality, that is, is an attribution, constructed as the act is constructed. Godzich, Foreward, to Pavel, *Poetics of Plot*, xxi–xxii.

20. Kenneth Burke, *The Rhetoric of Religion* (Berkeley and Los Angeles: University of California Press, 1970), 19. Philosophers are certainly not convinced that there can be any such thing as a negative act, since by definition the act is positive. Their concerns focus on how a negative act like not eating is relative to positive intentions. Unlike the negative in nature, that is, the negative in action is circumscribed by a construction of language whereby intentions, desires, and beliefs are often at odds with alternative descriptions and social meanings. Yet it is also bound by the possibilities of the nonexistence of the act. See, for example, Bruce Vermazen, "Negative Acts," in *Essays on Davidson: Actions and Events*, ed. Bruce Vermazen and Merrill B. Hintikka (Oxford: Clarendon Press, 1985), 93–104.

21. Through acting as through speaking, the subject becomes an object to itself; passive to its own acts; a self-division. Derrida says something similar in an early essay:

As soon as I speak, the words I have found (as soon as they are words) no longer belong to me, are originally *repeated*. . . . I must first hear myself. In soliloquy as in dialogue, to speak is to hear oneself. As soon as I am heard, as soon as I hear myself, the I who hears *itself*, becomes the I who speaks and takes speech from the I who thinks that he speaks and is heard in his own name.

Jacques Derrida, *Writing and Difference*, trans. Alan Bass (Chicago: University of Chicago Press, 1978), 177.

22. This, in fact, is what I believe George Herbert Mead implies when he says that "When a self does appear it always involves an experience of another; there could not be an experience of a self simply by itself" (*Mind, Self, and Society*, 1:195). Although Mead is writing in terms of a specific notion of society as the other, Derrida, quoted above, is simply extending that notion to the way that language itself is also inherited from the world as other rather than being simply, uniquely self-generated at each instance of speaking. An agent or subject in itself can be thus described as inhabited by a difference that keeps it from being identical to either itself or its acts, however much it may be responsible for them. A self appears as an identified (passive voice) cause. This does not necessarily mean that there is no person prior to an activity. It only alters the notion that the person is a sole and isolated origin of acts, that it is fully constituted and independent of context.

23. The radical philosophical discussion of this can be found in Schürmann's *Heidegger*. In this book he discusses a Heideggerian notion of action that is not based on "first principles" or a "rational *arche* that provides an anchorage for action." Such first principles, Schürmann says, perpetuate a focal point that is consistently deferred to an idealized image of a metaphysical site. An "an-archic" view instead tries to eliminate the focal points of both origins and telos. This anarchic principle is related to the "possibility" of nonbeing that is present in being. Later he says,

what is it that my existence makes its own in becoming authentic? My possibility of not being at all. Nothing, then, is made my own. Since he [Heidegger] retains "potential" and the "possible" as the decisive marks of authenticity, it is clear that the concept of authentic existence contains no teleological structure. Higher than *arche* and *telos* stand an-archy and a-teleocracy since "higher than actuality stands possibility." . . . Authentic temporality—not linear but ecstatic—abolishes representations of a "terminus a quo" and a "terminus ad quem" in the understanding of existence. (16)

24. "Language, to be emancipated, will have to rid itself of the grammar dictated by metaphysics. The tongue to be learned would then have to extricate itself from that fundamental *pros hen*, the subject-predicate attribution. . . . Either we learn to speak as the contemporary economy of presence speaks to us, or what is propitious in advanced technology will be lost. To put it negatively: either we unlearn the *pros hen* grammar, or the technological grip will be fatal for us. Either we listen and hear how the guiding word of Western philosophy, *eon* speaks to us today, or the accumulation of *onta* will consolidate their assault (*Andrang*)." Schürmann, *Heidegger*, 240–41.

25. Hannah Arendt, *The Human Condition* (Chicago: University of Chicago Press, 1958), 178.
26. Arendt, *Human Condition*, 184.
27. The active/passive duality structures a total view of action. But what is total about the act is not that it has *closure*, like a simple narrative, but that it is a recursive structure. That totality is both paradoxical and tautological. In Burke's example, the total act has a theological paradigm set forth in Lutheran doctrine.

> Christ's work on the Cross had the effect of changing God's attitude toward mankind, and . . . men born after the historical Christ can take advantage of this change. Here we have something like the conversion of God himself, brought about by Christ's sacrifice (a total action, a total passion). From the godlike nature came a godlike act that acted on God himself.

> Burke, *Grammar of Motives*, 19–20.

28. Beckett, *Waiting for Godot*, 58–59.
29. Maurice Merleau-Ponty, "Cezanne's Doubt," in *Sense and Non-Sense*, trans. Hubert L. Dreyfus and Patricia Allen Dreyfus (Evanston, Ill.: Northwestern University Press, 1964), 20–21.
30. See Paul Ricoeur, "Narrative Time," in *Critical Inquiry* 7, no.1 (autumn 1980): 169–90.
31. There is an image of this in Karel Reisz's film of the Harold Pinter screenplay for John Fowles's *The French Lieutenant's Woman*. In a movie within the movie, an actor is playing a character who is an amateur paleontologist; at one point we see him working with a shell in a stone. But it is impossible, visually, to determine whether he is uncovering it or sculpting it: the action is the same. Because at the same moment and in the same action Jeremy Irons is a paleontologist, a character, and an actor, because he is working both with and against the past of the shell to uncover or create it as it was, in a fiction and in an act for the camera, that filmic image captures the complexity of the active/passive, creator/ explorer, past/present conflations that are involved in doing and understanding what is done. Action itself conflates temporal categories as doing creates a done deed. The uncovering is a creating, or what the phenomenologist might call a bringing forth of that which is already there, creating the space of that which is already present. And that activity in some sense *makes* time more than taking it because it is an originating activity.
32. For example, in *An Essay concerning Technology*, Heidegger reformulates Aristotle's four causes (material, formal, final, and efficient) as categories not of *causes* but of "responsibility" to which an object is "indebted." He calls the categories not causes but "modes of occasioning" such that a silver chalice, which is his example, is not a final product but an "occa-

sion" that is indebted to the silver, the shape, the need for holding a sacramental liquid, and the silversmith. Martin Heidegger, *An Essay concerning Technology*, trans. William Lovitt (New York: Harper, 1971).

33. Martin Heidegger, "The Origin of the Work of Art," trans. Albert Hofstadter, in *Poetry, Language, Thought* (New York: Harper, 1971), 78.

Chapter 3

1. See James Calderwood, *If It Were Done: "Macbeth" and Tragic Action* (Amherst: University of Massachusetts Press, 1986): "In no other play do the words 'do,' 'done,' and 'deed' appear so often or so centrally. . . . And yet if the play is about action, about what is done, it is also about non-action, what is undone" (33).

2. All quotations from *Macbeth* are from the Arden Shakespeare, ed. Kenneth Muir (Cambridge: Harvard Univeristy Press, 1951).

3. See notes on this line in *Macbeth*, 12–13.

4. Kierkegaard writes of this spatial function of the accusative case in *Johannes Climacus:*

The Greek teacher presented grammar in a more philosophical way. When it was explained to Johannes that the accusative case, for example, is an extension in time and space, that the preposition does not govern the case but that the relation does, everything expanded before him. The preposition vanished; the extension in time and space became like an enormous empty picture for intuition.

Søren Kierkegaard, *Philosophical Fragments and Johannes Climacus*, ed. and trans. Howard V. Hong and Edna H. Hong, vol. 7 of *Kierkegaard's Writings* (Princeton: Princeton University Press, 1985), 121.

5. Bert States reminds me that in the film *Aliens 3*, wicked Lt. Ripley urges the monster to devour Sigourney Weaver with the line: "Just do what you do."

6. "The King hath happily receiv'd, Macbeth, / The news of thy success" (1.3.90–91); "They met me in the day of success; and I have learn'd by the perfect'st report, they have more in them than mortal knowledge" (1.5.1–3); "if th'assassination / Could trammel up the consequence, and catch / With his surcease success" (1.7.2–4).

7. William Empson, "Macbeth," in *Essays on Shakespeare* (Cambridge: Cambridge University Press, 1986), 141.

8. Bert O. States, "The Horses of *Macbeth*," *Kenyon Review* (spring 1985): 52–66.

9. Beckett, *Proust*, 1.

10. States, "The Horses of *Macbeth*," 56–57.

11. This is a classic actors' exercise in which partners start with one acting as a mirror for the other; in the course of the exercise, they switch back and forth with first one, then the other initiating the motions and the

other following. After a period of intense concentration upon each other, the two partners can end up performing motions that neither one initiates or follows. The motions nevertheless become simultaneous. The players lose the distinction between initiating and imitating and together generate a single motion.

12. René Girard, *To Double Business Bound* (Baltimore: Johns Hopkins University Press, 1978).

13. Maurice Merleau-Ponty, *The Visible and the Invisible*, trans. Alphonso Lingis (Evanston, Ill.: Northwestern University Press, 1968), 134–35.

14. Dowden, quoted by Kenneth Muir, *Macbeth*, n. 38, p. 15.

15. Empson, "Macbeth," 141.

16. From the excerpted Holinshed *Chronicle*, in *Macbeth*, 178.

17. Holinshed, 172.

18. Lacan, *Four Fundamental Concepts*, 53–64.

19. Terry Eagleton, *William Shakespeare* (Oxford: Basil Blackwell, 1986), 2.

20. Calderwood, *If It Were Done*, 42.

21. Lacan, *Four Fundamental Concepts*, 56.

22. Kierkegaard, *Johannes Climacus*, 142.

23. Paul Ricoeur, *Freedom and Nature*, trans. Erazim V. Kohák (Evanston, Ill.: Northwestern University Press, 1966), 163.

24. "Attention and process, understood in terms of each other, should give us a more complete understanding of the fundamental roles of imagination in the creation of decision. This in effect is the fundamental idea of analysis of motives, that all the forms of the involuntary are reflected in the imagination. This testing of values in imagination is here understood in terms of the universally imaginative character of attention. To pay attention is to see in a very broad, non-intellectualistic sense, that is, in a way to develop intuitively all the relations and all the values. Attention functions in the intuitive surroundings in which we try out most abstract values." Ricoeur, *Freedom and Nature*, 150.

25. "Attention is this very movement of observation which, in displacing itself, *changes* the mode of appearance of objects and their aspects. In effect, neither the world, nor even the least object, can be given all at once. Each object edges on actual perception, it is irrepressible. But the multiple attempts, the different faces or profiles which I must go through and name in order to posit the object in its unity, do not constitute an incoherent succession." Ricoeur, *Freedom and Nature*, 154.

26. "What I am suggesting is that Macbeth 'falls in evil' as other men fall in love. The murder of Duncan happens to him the way Juliet happens to Romeo. . . . I fetch the notion of demonic possession here not as the 'truth' about Macbeth's motivation—after all, ambition, 'manliness' and uxoriousness are operative as well—but to emphasize the extent to which Macbeth does not choose the murder but is chosen by it, well before he stages it as an act in which he as well as Duncan is victimized." Calderwood, *If It Were Done*, 49 and 51.

27. A paper by Eric Raneletti, an undergraduate student, provided one of the best summaries of this idea. In the analysis of the "If it were done" speech he wrote: "Macbeth contemplates the future as if it were already planned by chance."

28. Christa Wolf, *Cassandra*, trans. Jan Van Heurck (New York: Farrar, Straus, Giroux, 1984), 144.

29. Roland Barthes, "The Structure of the Fait-divers," trans. Richard Howard, in *Critical Essays* (Evanston, Ill.: Northwestern University Press, 1972), 193.

30. "We may discern a dramatistic pun, involving a merger of active and passive in the expression, 'the motivation of an act.' Strictly speaking, the act of an agent would be the movement not of one *moved* but of a *mover.* . . . For an act is by definition active, whereas to be moved (or motivated) is by definition passive. . . . We could state the paradox another way by saying that the concept of activation implies a kind of passive-behind-the-passive; for an agent who is 'motivated by his passions' would be 'moved by his being-movedness,' or 'acted upon by his state of being acted upon.'" Burke, *Grammar of Motives*, 40.

31. Burke, *Grammar of Motives*, 14.

32. "In order to escape the systematization and domination of rationality, the self must be fully lost in immanence in order to establish the whole man . . . as a completely unsubordinated realm. . . . The self is no longer subject, but sovereign. And communication is no longer a teleological activity, but rather a function of both love and evil where the relation between two beings is put entirely at risk, exposed to the vagaries of chance." Allen S. Weiss, *The Aesthetics of Excess* (Albany: State University of New York Press, 1989), 20. "Klossowski demands the loss of self; Bataille demands the self as loss. Yet in both cases, the Eternal Return signifies a unique, heterogeneous, ultimately incommunicable experience, which is an enrichment of the 'here and now' through the affirmation of chance" (21).

33. Weiss, *Aesthetics of Excess*, 19.

34. "Let us leave textual criticism to graduate students, formal criticism to esthetes, and recognize that what has been said is not still to be said; that an expression does not have the same value twice, does not live two lives; that all words, once spoken, are dead and function only at the moment when they are uttered, that a form, once it has served, cannot be used again and asks only to be replaced by another, and that the theater is the only place in the world where a gesture, once made, can never be made the same way twice." Antonin Artaud, *The Theater and Its Double*, trans. Mary Caroline Richards (New York: Grove Press, 1958), 75.

35. Artaud, *Theater and Its Double*, 78.

36. Artaud, *Theater and Its Double*, 79. Later, he says,

I have therefore said "cruelty" as I might have said "life" or "necessity," because I want to indicate especially that for me the theater is act and perpetual emanation, that there is nothing congealed about it, that I turn it into a true act, hence living, magical. . . . We need true action, but without practical consequence. It is not on the social level that the action of theater unfolds. Still less on the moral and psychological levels. (114–15)

37. As Derrida writes of Artaud's theater:

The stage, certainly, *will no longer represent*, since it will not operate as an addition, as the sensory illustration of a text already written, thought, or lived outside the stage, which the stage would then only repeat but whose fabric it would not constitute. The stage will no longer operate as the repetition of a *present*, will no longer re-present a present that would exist elsewhere and prior to it, a present whose plenitude would be older than it, absent from it, and rightfully capable of doing without it: the being-present-to-itself of the absolute Logos, the living present of God.

Jacques Derrida, "The Theatre of Cruelty," in *Writing and Difference*, 237.

38. For a telling story about Lacan and these interests, see Catherine Clément, *The Lives and Legends of Jacques Lacan*, trans. Arthur Goldhammer (New York: Columbia University Press, 1983), 53–101.

39. "These metaphors of adhesion [to accept certain reasons; to adhere to a point of view; to go along with an opinion; to adopt a position] reveal that there is a point of passivity or of receptivity in the heart of volition by which will renders itself sensitive to anything which can incline it without necessitating it, which can provide it with an impulsion and a legitimization. It is a proper characteristic of finite liberty to be able to decide only by becoming sensitive to motives." The passage continues, significantly:

But if motivation represents the moment of passivity of will, in return the relation of motive to volition gives to the human body a completely original significance. Our needs, our desires are not simply irresistible forces that can be measured and treated as physical magnitudes; they are also significations, evaluations, which are capable of entering into a field of motivation and of being confronted there with other values (esthetic, moral, religious, etc.).

Paul Ricoeur, "Volition and Action," in *Phenomenology of Will and Action: Lexington Conference on Pure and Applied Phenomenology*, ed. Erwin W. Strauss and Richard M. Griffith (Pittsburgh: Duquesne University Press, 1967), 24.

40. Heidegger tries to situate a similar unity between hand and thought in *What Is Called Thinking?* where he points out that any separation between

the work of the hand and that of thinking is the result of a metaphysical notion of thought:

the hand's gestures run everywhere through language, in their most perfect purity precisely when man speaks by being silent. And only when man speaks, does he think—not the other way around, as metaphysics still believes. Every motion of the hand in every one of its works carries itself through the element of thinking, every bearing of the hand bears itself in that element. All the work of the hand is rooted in thinking. (16)

41. Herbert Blau, *The Audience* (Baltimore: Johns Hopkins University Press, 1990), 61.
42. Merleau-Ponty, *Visible and Invisible*, 135.

Chapter 4

1. Bert O. States, *Irony and Drama* (Ithaca, N. Y.: Cornell University Press, 1971), 96.
2. The inability to act and the characterization of the traditional hero as victim is particular, according to George Lukács, to modern drama. It is a historical phenomenon in dramatic literature that places "man as merely the intersection point of great forces, and his deeds not even his own" ("Sociology of Modern Drama," 430). Describing the change in form and content that marks modern drama, Peter Szondi also remarks that "Action gives way to that conditionality of which humankind is the powerless victim." Peter Szondi, *Theory of the Modern Drama*, trans. Michael Hays, Theory and History of Literature Series, vol. 29, (Minneapolis: University of Minnesota Press, 1987), 45. And in Chekhov in particular, he says, "The double renunciation that marks Chekhov's characters seems inevitably to necessitate the abandonment of action and dialogue—the two most important formal categories of the Drama and, thus, dramatic form itself" (19). Inaction as both a formal attribute and a mark of modern character is without doubt a significant historical phenomenon, though given the case of *Hamlet* it is also a thematic category.
3. Michael Frayn translation of Anton Chekhov, *Three Sisters* (London: Methuen, 1983). The differences between Frayn's translation and Ann Dunnigan's in *Chekhov: The Major Plays* (New York: New American Library, 1964) are significant, though not at this point.
4. Chekhov, *Three Sisters*, Frayn translation, 1.
5. Chekhov, *Three Sisters*, Dunnigan translation, 238.
6. Ricoeur, *Freedom and Nature*, 201.
7. Chekhov, *Three Sisters*, Frayn translation, 89.
8. I thank Zander Brietzke for pointing out this distinction to me. The grammar source is Charles E. Townsend, *Continuing Russian* SLAVICA, 1980–81, 105–8.

9. Arendt, *Human Condition*, 80.

10. Elaine Scarry, *The Body in Pain: The Making and Unmaking of the World* (Oxford: Oxford University Press, 1985), 169.

11. At this point, there are important differences in English translations. Dunnigan translates: "Our brother will probably become a professor; in any case, he won't go on living here. So there's nothing to stop us but poor Masha." Frayn translates: "Our brother will most likely be a professor. All the same, he won't want to live here. The only one who's stuck here is poor Masha." In Dunnigan, Masha is an obstacle to their leaving, which prompts Olga to say she can at least visit in the summers and therefore is not a real obstacle. In Frayn's translation, Masha presents no obstacle but seems to deserve pity for being stuck; sympathy for her unpleasantly married condition can be mitigated by having her visit. In either case, Masha is not a separable part of the family unit.

12. By the second act, when she appears as actually having been working, Irina says, "I shall have to look for another job—this one's not for me. What I so longed for, what I dreamed of, are the very things it doesn't have. It's work with no poetry in it, mindless labour." Work as poetry, in other words, is a replacement for the loss of the image that working entails. Poetry now becomes the idealized image that overcomes actuality. Work is as much an image as Moscow. Work and the imperative to work, in this case, are not exactly identical to Moscow, but are misperceived in an identical way.

13. The dissertation of Zander Brietzke, "Nothing Is but What Is Not: Chekhovian Drama and the Crisis of Representation" (Ph.D. diss., Stanford University, 1992) develops the idea of the physical marginality of the family estate in Chekhov's plays. He explores the implications of how such marginality serves the question of realism in theatrical representation as an act of being there and not there at the same time.

14. Jacques Lacan, "Function and Field of Speech and Language," in *Écrits*, 104.

15. Richard Rorty, *Contingency, Irony, and Solidarity* (Cambridge: Cambridge University Press, 1989), 105.

16. Chekhov, *Three Sisters*, Dunnigan translation, 286.

17. Wilshire, *Role Playing and Identity*, 124–25.

18. Ricoeur, *Freedom and Nature*, 411.

19. Brietzke's dissertation, "Nothing Is But," also details the significant elements of Chekhov's dramaturgy that contradict the idea that his realism is simply a duplicate of a real world. He thoroughly illustrates the performative and theatrical elements that comprise the artificiality of Chekhov's techniques.

20. Chekhov, *Three Sisters*, Dunnigan translation, 268.

21. Chekhov, *Three Sisters*, Dunnigan translation, 239.

22. Chekhov, *Three Sisters*, Dunnigan translation, 241.

23. Chekhov, *Three Sisters*, Dunnigan translation, 276.

24. Chekhov, *Three Sisters*, Dunnigan translation, 271.

25. Peter Bitsilli, *Chekhov's Art: A Stylistic Analysis,* trans. Toby W. Clyman and Edwina Cruise (Ann Arbor: Ardis, 1983).
26. Charles W. Meister, *Chekhov Criticism: 1880 through 1986* (Jefferson, N.C.: MacFarland, 1988), 7.
27. My thanks to B. States for pointing out the connection.
28. Mikhail Lermontov, *A Hero of Our Time,* trans. Vladimir Nabokov (New York: Doubleday, 1958), 123.
29. Chekhov, *Three Sisters,* Dunnigan translation, 337.
30. S. E. Gontarski, "The Intent of Undoing," in *Samuel Beckett,* ed. Harold Bloom (New York: Chelsea House, 1985), 242.
31. In discussing the characters of Hamm and Clov, Charles R. Lyons says:

> These unelaborated references suggest that the relationship holds a variety of socio-political and psychological dimensions. The notion of rounds and paupers indicates an extensive ownership of property, and the denial of Clov's bicycle points towards a capricious bestowal and refusal of favours—the kind of arbitrary benevolence and cruelty that engenders acute resentment as well as obligation in its victims.

Samuel Beckett (London: Macmillan, 1983), 56.
32. Ruby Cohn, *Just Play: Beckett's Theater* (Princeton: Princeton University Press, 1980), 3.
33. For *Film,* Beckett continues:

> All extraneous perception suppressed, animal, human, divine, self-perception maintains in being.
>   Search of non-being in flight from extraneous perception breaking down in inescapability of self-perception.
>   No truth value attaches to above, regarded as of merely structural and dramatic convenience.

Samuel Beckett, *Film,* in *Collected Shorter Plays* (New York; Grove, 1984), 163.
34. Gadamer, *Truth and Method,* 97.
35. "The signifier is the death of festival," says Derrida in his critique of Rousseau. But the festival, which is a natural occurrence to Rousseau where "each sees and loves himself in the others so that all will be better united," is for Derrida "without object, without sacrifice, without expense, and without play. Above all without masks. It has no outside although it takes place out of doors. It maintains itself in a purely interior relation to itself." Jacques Derrida, *Of Grammatology,* trans. Gayatri Chakrovorty Spivak (Baltimore: Johns Hopkins University Press, 1976), 306–7.
36. Richard M. Griffith, "Simulation and Dissimulation" in Strauss and Griffith, *Phenomenology of Will and Action,* 237. One of Griffith's more startling suggestions in psychological terms is that the ability to put on play roles and put on social masks is a mode of healthy self-knowledge and that

because a schizophrenic personality cannot account for multiplicity, "the schizophrenic cannot act" (247).

Schizophrenics have one thing in common, we say they are "not themselves." They don't play the script of their once character, a character similar enough to ours for us to understand them. I *have* my roles, reject the notion that I am them (God is no respecter of "person"). . . . to be possessed is to be dis-possessed; the possessed would have nothing left to call his own. I am master of my role, the role which belongs to me as a type of possession. The schizophrenic has lost his roles, those which are similar to ours, and hence, neither does he "belong." (247–48)

37. Wilshire, *Role Playing and Identity*, 185.

Chapter 5

1. Jacques Lacan articulates the relation between image, language, and the Freudian notion of the Ideal-Ego in his famous essay, "The Mirror Stage."

   This form would have to be called the Ideal-I, if we wished to incorporate it into our usual register, in the sense that it will also be the source of secondary identifications. . . . this form situates the agency of the ego, before its social determination, in a fictional direction, which will always remain irreducible for the individual. (In *Écrits*, 2)
2. Gilbert Ryle, *The Concept of Mind* (Chicago: University of Chicago Press, 1949), 30.
3. Saltz in his dissertation "Theatre Event" has developed an extensive argument for the use of game criteria in understanding the reality of action on the stage in both practical and theoretical ways. The criteria answer both logical and aesthetic questions about the ontology of the theater event in comparison with other art forms, and Saltz's work is the most comprehensive and rigorous discussion I know of. Saltz takes the argument far beyond what I am touching upon here and shows the implications of using game theory in concrete ways.
4. This notion of the act appears in various contexts: from Cassirer's idea that symbols are a culture's articulation of experience; to Kenneth Burke's idea of language as symbolic action; to the anthropology of Clifford Geertz; to Paul Ricoeur's view that "if human action can be narrated, it is because it is always already articulated by signs, rules and norms" (Ricoeur, *Time and Narrative*, 1:57).
5. Lacan, *Four Fundamental Concepts*, 50–51.
6. Lacan, *Four Fundamental Concepts*, 53–64. This is the section in which Lacan discusses "tuché and automaton" and the position of the subject "between perception and consciousness."

7. Constantin Stanislavski, *An Actor Prepares*, trans. Elizabeth Reynolds Hapgood (New York: Theatre Arts, 1948), 120–53. Stanislavski, of course, is clear about the difference between a "plane of actual fact" and the theatrical act that "originates on the plane of imaginative and artistic fiction" (121). "Truth on the stage is whatever we can believe in with sincerity, whether in ourselves or in our colleagues" (122). While noting the difference between a real-world act and a theatrical one, he would apparently insist upon the reality of the stage event (see Saltz, "Theatre Event").

8. This is a chapter heading in Ryle's *Concept of Mind*. While the distinction seems perfectly obvious, Ryle is making a specific case to deny the occult aspect of the mind/body paradigm in the post-Cartesian world. He insists that the mind is not a separate world and that knowing is not a secret, interior dimension apart from and holier than public practice.

It should be noticed that the boy is not said to know how to play, if all that he can do is to recite the rules accurately. He must be able to make the required moves. But he is said to know how to play if, although he cannot cite the rules, he normally does make the permitted moves, avoid the forbidden moves and protest if his opponent makes forbidden moves. His knowledge *how* is exercised primarily in the moves that he makes, or concedes, and in the moves that he avoids or vetoes." (40)

9. Levin, *Question of Hamlet*, 111.

10. "The anonymous 'This' becomes the unique 'I,' who is part of the paternally shared 'Hamlet,' who merges with the universal 'Dane.' During the middle of the play Hamlet could have gone no further than to say 'This is I.' Now, as he is about to descend with Laertes into the grave and invite death, the presence of all three terms implied the accommodation of the confirmed self within a universal context." James Calderwood, *To Be and Not to Be: Negation and Metadrama in "Hamlet."* (New York: Columbia University Press, 1983), 40–41.

11. See this sense of the Symbolic in Jacques Lacan, "Desire and the Interpretation of Desire in *Hamlet*," trans. James Hulbert, in *Literature and Psychoanalysis*, ed. Shoshana Felman (Baltimore: Johns Hopkins University Press, 1982), 11–52.

12. Burke, *Grammar of Motives*, 66.

13. Calderwood, *To Be*, 5.

14. Arendt, *Human Condition*, 176–77.

15. Beckett, *Waiting for Godot*, 24.

16. Charles Altieri says,

On the one hand, the values inherent in a dramatistic approach are not easily reconciled with any type of structuralist formalism, and, on the other, they challenge the often disputed but by now almost standard tendency in the social sciences to imagine that adequate explanations of human behavior must take the form of causal laws on a scientific model. (*Act and Quality*, 99)

An example of a scientist taking a "dramatistic" approach to neurological problems is Oliver Sachs in his popular book, *The Man Who Mistook His Wife for a Hat*.

17. "When Christ said, 'I am the way' (*hodos*), we could translate, 'I am the act,' or more fully, 'I represent a system, or synthesis, or the right acts.' *Tao* and *yoga* are similar words for act. And we see how readily act in this sense can overlap upon agency when we consider our ordinary attitude towards scientific method (*met-hodos*), which we think of pragmatically, not as a way of life, or *act* of *being*, but as a *means* of *doing*." Burke, *Grammar of Motives*, 15.

18. Both essays, "The Third Meaning" and "The Grain of the Voice" are in Barthes, *Image-Music-Text*.

19. Ricoeur discusses the textuality of action in terms of four features of discourse: the objectification that has the structure of a locutionary act with propositional content; the detachment of the act from its agents that gives the act the appearance of a consciousness of its own because of its social dimension; the development of significance beyond its initial conditions; and openness of it as a work to new interpretations and meanings as it is addressed to the world. Like a speech act, it has the dimensions of the act *of* saying; of what is done *in* saying; and of what is done *by* saying. See Paul Ricoeur, "The Model of the Text," in *Hermeneutics and the Human Sciences*, ed. and trans. John B. Thompson (Cambridge: Cambridge University Press, 1981), 197–221.

20. A quotation from Paul Ricoeur's *The Rule of Metaphor* (Toronto: University of Toronto Press, 1977), 248, may help define the issue. In discussing Cassirer's notion that language does not distinguish between the relational and existential senses of the verb *to be*, Ricoeur asks,

But is there not a metaphorical sense of the verb to be itself, in which the same tension would be preserved that we found first between words (between "nature" and "temple"), then between two interpretations (the literal and the metaphorical), and finally between identity and difference? . . . In order to elucidate this tension deep within the logical force of the verb *to be*, we must expose an "is not" itself implied in the impossibility of the literal interpretation, yet present as a filigree in the metaphorical "is." . . . Does not the tension that affects the copula in its relational function also affect the copula in its existential function?

21. C. W. Nevius, "In Short, It Was a Splendid Moment," *San Francisco Chronicle*, 2 May 1987, sec. D. The article concerns the heroics of Purvis Short. See Gadamer's phrase, "in spending oneself on the task of the game, one is, in fact, playing oneself out" (*Truth and Method*, 97).

22. Calderwood, *To Be*, 23.
23. Marion Trousdale, *Shakespeare and the Rhetoricians* (Chapel Hill: University of North Carolina Press, 1982).
24. Gadamer, *Truth and Method*, 94.
25. This description derives in part from Reiner Schürmann's discussion of a "displacement of responsibility from the moral to the economic," taking Heidegger's idea that "at the heart of the metaphysical concept of responsibility lies a call for accountability. The claiming of responsibility for one's action in his terms is a response to the call of difference . . . between world and thing." When Schürmann uses the term he is noting the shift from a human-centered notion that places human agency and essence as the origin of a world to a worldly manifold in which agents act and respond to the conditions that always already are. Responsibility in his terms is not an assessment of the ownership of an action in the terms that tribunal laws or a legislature (whether internal or external) might determine. Rather, like language, responsibility is a "response to the historical modifications of the event . . . to the economy that calls upon them. . . . The event of presencing 'uses' men, it situates them in such a way that everything they undertake is but a response to the economy that calls upon them" (263). Irresponsibility is not a breach of laws but a "refusal to answer the summons." In Kenneth Burke's terms, this might be akin to refusal to will one's fall, whereas the joining of the old notion of will to the event of gravity is an act of taking responsibility for what happens. And such taking of responsibility is a mark of "character." Schürmann, *Heidegger*, 262–63.
26. Gadamer, *Truth and Method*, 95–96.
27. This is the argument throughout Calderwood's *To Be*.
28. Beckett, *Waiting for Godot*, 25.
29. The expanded quotation reads:

> As something disclosed, Dasein exists factically in the way of *Being with Others*. It maintains itself in an intelligibility which is public and average. When the "now that . . ." and the "then when . . ." have been interpreted and expressed in our everyday Being with one another, they will be understood in principle, even though their dating is unequivocal only within certain limits. In the "most intimate" Being-with-one-another of several people, they can say *"now"* and say it "together," though each of them gives a different date to the "now" which he is saying: "now that this or that has come to pass . . ." The "now" which anyone expresses is always said in the publicness of Being-in-the-world with one another. Thus the time which any Dasein has currently interpreted and expressed has as such already been *given a public character* on the basis of that Dasein's ecstatical Being-in-the-world. In so far, then, as everyday concern understands itself in terms of the "world" of its concern and takes its "time," it does *not* know this "time" *as its own*, but concernfully *utilizes* the time which "there is" ["es gibt"]—the time with which "they"

reckon. Indeed the publicness of "time" is all the more compelling, the more *explicitly* factical Dasein *concerns* itself with time in specifically taking it into its reckoning.

Martin Heidegger, *Being and Time*, trans. John Macquarrie and Edward Robinson (New York: Harper and Row, 1962), 2.6.79.411, pp. 463–64.

30. Just for comparison, it might be helpful to notice the way that the film medium can in fact objectify time, can make it appear as an object. As Gilles Deleuze has shown, film can create a "time image" that appears to be independent of the motions of bodies and is not merely a measurement and segmentation of the movement of bodies. Rather than time measuring the movement of bodies, that is, figures and images on the screen are means of constructing "time" itself. The filmic eye can regard the way in which time inhabits objects as opposed to objects inhabiting time. In this sense, both *Hamlet* and *Waiting for Godot* could be understood as similarly filmic: each in its way makes time appear as both duration and present, equally dependent upon the agents and the viewer. Film requires no social contract or agreement about now because of its mechanistic fatality: the fatality that is also both duration and present. It does not exhibit any friction between the name of the act, in an original text, and the enactment. Through the image it has the capacity (in specific cases discussed by Deleuze) to make time visible. If time is not specifically visible in either *Hamlet* or *Godot*, it is nonetheless perceptible *as* time in its multiple dimensions.

31. Beckett, *Waiting for Godot*, 24.

32. Burke, *Grammar of Motives*, 245.

Bibliography

Altieri, Charles. *Act and Quality: A Theory of Literary Meaning and Humanistic Understanding*. Amherst: University of Massachusetts Press, 1981.

Arendt, Hannah. *The Human Condition*. Chicago: University of Chicago Press, 1958.

Aristotle. *The Complete Works of Aristotle*. Ed. Jonathan Barnes. Bollingen Series no. 71. Princeton: Princeton University Press, 1984.

Artaud, Antonin. *The Theater and Its Double*. Trans. Mary Caroline Richards. New York: Grove Press, 1958.

Barthes, Roland. *Image-Music-Text*. Trans. Stephen Heath. New York: Hill and Wang, 1977.

——. *The Pleasure of the Text*. Trans. Richard Miller. New York: Hill and Wang, 1973.

——. "The Structure of the Fait-divers." Trans. Richard Howard. In *Critical Essays*. Evanston, Ill.: Northwestern University Press, 1972.

Beaune, Jean-Claude. "The Classical Age of Automate: An Impressionistic Survey from the Sixteenth to the Nineteenth Century." In *Fragments for a History of the Human Body*, ed. Michel Feher, Ramona Naddaff, and Nadia Tazi. New York: Zone, 1989.

Beckett, Samuel. *Film*. In *Collected Shorter Plays*. New York: Grove Press, 1984.

——. *Proust*. New York: Grove Press, 1957.

——. *Waiting for Godot*. New York: Grove Press, 1954.

Benjamin, Walter. "The Storyteller: Reflections on the Works of Nikolai Leskov." In *Illuminations*, ed. Hannah Arendt, trans. Harry Zohn. New York: Schocken Books, 1969.

Benveniste, Emile. *Problems in General Linguistics*. Trans. Mary Elizabeth Meek. Miami Linguistics Series. Coral Gables: University of Miami Press, 1971.

Bitsilli, Peter. *Chekhov's Art: A Stylistic Analysis*. Trans. Toby W. Clyman and Edwina Cruise. Ann Arbor: Ardis, 1983.

Blau, Herbert. *The Audience*. Baltimore: Johns Hopkins University Press, 1991.

Brewer, Maria Minich. "A Loosening of Tongues: From Narrative Economy to Women Writing." *MLN* (December 1984): 1141–61.

Brietzke, Zander. "Nothing Is but What Is Not: Chekhovian Drama and the Crisis of Representation." Ph.D. diss., Stanford University, 1992.

Brooks, Peter. *Reading for the Plot*. New York: Vintage, 1984.

Burke, Kenneth. *A Grammar of Motives*. Berkeley and Los Angeles: University of California Press, 1969.

———. "On Piety." In *Permanence and Change*. Indianapolis: Bobbs-Merrill, 1965.

———. *The Rhetoric of Religion*. Berkeley and Los Angeles: University of California Press, 1970.

Butler, Judith. *Gender Trouble: Feminism and the Subversion of Identity*. New York: Routledge, 1990.

Calderwood, James L. *If It Were Done: "Macbeth" and Tragic Action*. Amherst: University of Massachusetts Press, 1986.

———. *To Be and Not to Be: Negation and Metadrama in "Hamlet."* New York: Columbia University Press, 1983.

Chatman, Seymour. "What Novels Can Do That Films Can't (and Vice Versa)." *Critical Inquiry* 7, no. 1 (autumn 1980): 121–40.

Chekhov, Anton. *Chekhov: The Major Plays*. Trans. Ann Dunnigan. New York: New American Library, 1964.

———. *The Three Sisters*. Trans. Michael Frayn. London: Methuen, 1983.

Clément, Catherine. *The Lives and Legends of Jacques Lacan*. Trans. Arthur Goldhammer. New York: Columbia University Press, 1983.

Cohn, Ruby. *Just Play: Beckett's Theater*. Princeton: Princeton University Press, 1980.

Danto, Arthur C. *Analytic Philosophy of Action*. Cambridge: Cambridge University Press, 1973.

de Lauretis, Teresa. *Alice Doesn't: Feminism, Semiotics, Cinema*. Bloomington: Indiana University Press, 1982.

Deleuze, Gilles. "The Schizophrenic and Language." In *Textual Strategies*, ed. and trans. Josué V. Harari. Ithaca, N. Y.: Cornell University Press, 1979.

Derrida, Jacques. *Of Grammatology*. Trans. Gayatri Chakrovorty Spivak. Baltimore: Johns Hopkins University Press, 1976.

———. *Writing and Difference*. Trans. Alan Bass. Chicago: University of Chicago Press, 1978.

Eagleton, Terry. *William Shakespeare*. Oxford: Basil Blackwell, 1986.

Empson, William. "Macbeth." In *Essays on Shakespeare*. Cambridge: Cambridge University Press, 1986.

Féral, Josette. "What Is Left of Performance Art? Autopsy of a Function: Birth of a Genre." *Discourse* 14, no.2 (spring 1992): 142–62.

Gadamer, Hans-Georg. *Truth and Method*. Trans. Garrett Barden and John Cumming. New York: Crossroad, 1986.

Geertz, Clifford. *Local Knowledge: Further Essays in Interpretive Anthropology*. New York: Basic Books, 1983.

———. *Works and Lives: The Anthropologist as Author*. Stanford: Stanford University Press, 1988.

Girard, René. *To Double Business Bound*. Baltimore: Johns Hopkins University Press, 1978.

Gontarski, S. E. "The Intent of Undoing." In *Samuel Beckett*, ed. Harold Bloom. New York: Chelsea House, 1985.

Griffith, Richard M. "Simulation and Dissimulation." In *Phenomenology of Will and Action: Lexington Conference on Pure and Applied Phenomenology*, ed. Erwin W. Straus and Richard M. Griffith. Pittsburgh: Duquesne University Press, 1967.

Haar, Michel. "Nietzsche and Metaphysical Language." In *The New Nietzsche: Contemporary Styles of Interpretation*, ed. David Allison. New York: Delta, 1977.

Handke, Peter. "Offending the Audience." In *Kaspar and Other Plays*, trans. Michael Roloff. New York: Grove, 1969.

Harari, Josué, ed. *Textual Strategies*. Ithaca, N.Y.: Cornell University Press, 1979.

Hartwig, Joan. *Shakespeare's Analogical Scene*. Lincoln: University of Nebraska Press, 1983.

Heidegger, Martin. *Being and Time*. Trans. John Macquarrie and Edward Robinson. New York: Harper and Row, 1962.

———. *An Essay concerning Technology*. Trans. William Lovitt. New York: Harper, 1971.

———. "The Origin of the Work of Art." Trans. Albert Hofstadter. In *Poetry, Language, Thought*. New York: Harper, 1971.

———. *What Is Called Thinking?* Trans. J. Glenn Gray. New York: Harper and Row, 1968.

Hernadi, Paul. "Doing, Making, Meaning: Toward a Theory of Verbal Practice." *PMLA* 103, no. 5 (October 1988): 749–58.

Iser, Wolfgang. *The Fictive and the Imaginary: Charting Literary Anthropology*. Baltimore: Johns Hopkins University Press, 1993.

Kenny, Anthony. *Action, Emotion, and Will*. London: Routledge and Kegan Paul, 1963.

Kermode, Frank. *The Sense of an Ending*. New York: Oxford University Press, 1967

Kierkegaard, Søren. *Philosophical Fragments and Johannes Climacus*. Ed. and trans. Howard V. Hong and Edna H. Hong. Vol. 7 of *Kierkegaard's Writings*. Princeton: Princeton University Press, 1985.

Lacan, Jacques. "Desire and the Interpretation of Desire in Hamlet." trans. James Hulbert. In *Literature and Psychoanalysis*, ed. Shoshana Felman. Baltimore: Johns Hopkins University Press, 1982.

———. *Écrits*. Trans. Alan Sheridan. New York: Norton, 1977.

———. *The Four Fundamental Concepts of Psychoanalysis*. Trans. Alan Sheridan. Ed. Jacques Alain Miller. New York: Norton, 1981.

Lanser, Susan S. "Toward a Feminist Narratology." *Style* 20 (fall 1986): 341–59.

Lermontov, Mihail. *A Hero of Our Time*. Trans. Vladimir Nabokov. New York: Doubleday, 1958.

Levin, Harry. *The Question of Hamlet*. Oxford: Oxford University Press, 1959.

Lukács, Georg. "The Sociology of Modern Drama." Trans. Lee Baxandall. In

The Theory of the Modern Stage, ed. Eric Bentley. Harmondsworth, England: Penguin, 1968.

Lyons, Charles R. *Samuel Beckett*. London: Macmillan, 1983.

Mead, George Herbert. *Mind, Self, and Society*. Ed. Charles W. Morris. Chicago: University of Chicago Press, 1934.

Meister, Charles W. *Chekhov Criticism: 1880 through 1986*. Jefferson, N.C.: MacFarland, 1988.

Merleau-Ponty, Maurice. "Cezanne's Doubt." In *Sense and Non-Sense*, trans. Hubert L. Dreyfus and Patricia Allen Dreyfus. Evanston, Ill.: Northwestern University Press, 1964.

———. *The Phenomenology of Perception*. Trans. Colin Smith. London: Routledge, 1962.

———. *The Visible and the Invisible*. Ed. Colin Lefort. Trans. Alphonso Lingis. Evanston, Ill.: Northwestern University Press, 1968.

Mitchell, W. J. T., ed. *On Narrative*. Special issue of *Critical Inquiry* 7, no. 1 (autumn 1980).

Nietzsche, Friedrich. *On the Genealogy of Morals*. Trans. Walter Kaufmann. New York: Vintage, 1969.

Paska, Roman. "The Inanimate Incarnate." In *Fragments for a History of the Human Body*, ed. Michel Feher, Ramona Naddaff, and Nadia Tazi. New York: Zone, 1989.

Pavel, Thomas G. *The Poetics of Plot: The Case of English Renaissance Drama*. Foreward by Wlad Godzich. Minneapolis: University of Minnesota Press, 1985.

Ricoeur, Paul. *Freedom and Nature*. Trans. Erazim V. Kohák. Evanston, Ill.: Northwestern University Press, 1966.

———. "The Model of the Text." In *Hermeneutics and the Human Sciences*, ed. and trans. John B. Thompson. Cambridge: Cambridge University Press, 1981.

———. "Narrative Time." *Critical Inquiry* 7, no. 1 (autumn 1980): 169–90.

———. *The Rule of Metaphor*. Toronto: University of Toronto Press, 1977.

———. *Time and Narrative*. Trans. Kathleen McLaughlin and David Pellauer. 3 vols. Chicago: University of Chicago Press, 1984–88.

———. "Volition and Action." In *Phenomenology of Will and Action: Lexington Conference on Pure and Applied Phenomenology*, ed. Erwin W. Straus and Richard M. Griffith. Pittsburgh: Duquesne University Press, 1967.

Ricoeur, Paul, and Hans-Georg Gadamer. "The Conflict of Interpretations." In *Phenomenology: Dialogues and Bridges*, ed. Ronald Bruzina and Bruce Wilshire. Albany: State University of New York Press, 1982.

Rorty, Richard. *Contingency, Irony, and Solidarity*. Cambridge: Cambridge University Press, 1989.

Ryle, Gilbert. *The Concept of Mind*. Chicago: University of Chicago Press, 1949.

Saltz, David Zucker. "The Reality of the Theatre Event: Logical Foundations of Dramatic Performance." Ph.D. diss., Stanford University, 1992.

Scarry, Elaine. *The Body in Pain: The Making and Unmaking of the World*. Oxford: Oxford University Press, 1985.

Schmitt, Natalie Crohn. *Actors and Onlookers: Theater and Twentieth Century Views of Nature*. Evanston, Ill.: Northwestern University Press, 1990.

Schürmann, Reiner. *Heidegger on Being and Acting: From Principles to Anarchy*. Bloomington: Indiana University Press, 1987.

Shakespeare, William. *Macbeth*. Ed. Kenneth Muir. The Arden Shakespeare. Cambridge: Harvard University Press, 1951.

———. *The Riverside Shakespeare*. Boston: Houghton Mifflin, 1974.

Stanislavski, Constantin. *An Actor Prepares*. Trans. Elizabeth Reynolds Hapgood. New York: Theatre Arts, 1948.

States, Bert O. *"Hamlet" and the Concept of Character*. Baltimore: Johns Hopkins University Press, 1992.

———. "The Horses of *Macbeth*." *Kenyon Review* (spring 1985): 52–66.

———. *Irony and Drama*. Ithaca, N.Y.: Cornell University Press, 1971.

Szondi, Peter. *Theory of the Modern Drama*. Trans. Michael Hays. Theory and History of Literature Series. Vol. 29. Minneapolis: University of Minnesota Press, 1987.

Trimpi, Wesley. *Muses of One Mind: The Literary Analysis of Experience and Its Continuity*. Princeton: Princeton University Press, 1983.

Trousdale, Marion. *Shakespeare and the Rhetoricians*. Chapel Hill: University of North Carolina Press, 1982.

Vermazen, Bruce. "Negative Acts." In *Essays on Davidson: Actions and Events*, ed. Bruce Vermazen and Merrill B. Hintikka. Oxford: Clarendon Press, 1985.

Weiss, Allen S. *The Aesthetics of Excess*. Albany: State University of New York Press, 1989.

White, Hayden. "The Value of Narrativity in the Representation of Reality." *Critical Inquiry* 7, no. 1 (autumn 1980): 5–27.

Wilshire, Bruce. *Role Playing and Identity: The Limits of Theatre as Metaphor*. Bloomington: Indiana University Press, 1982.

———. "Theatre as Phenomenology: The Disclosure of Historical Life." In *Phenomenology: Dialogues and Bridges*, ed. Ronald Bruzina and Bruce Wilshire. Albany: State University of New York Press, 1982.

Wittgenstein, Ludwig. *Philosophical Investigations*. Trans. G. E. M. Anscombe. New York: Macmillan, 1953.

Wolf, Christa. *Cassandra*. Trans. Jan Van Heurck. New York: Farrar, Straus, Giroux, 1984.

Index